THE DANCE PROGRAM

A Series of Publications in the Field of Dance and the Related Arts

Volumes in Preparation

On Tap Dancing, by Paul Draper, *edited and compiled by Fran Avallone*

Olga Preobrazhenskaya, a biography, by Elvira Roné, *translated by Fernau Hall*

Ballerina, a biography of Violette Verdy, by Victoria Huckenpahler

The Bournonville School (in four volumes), including music and notation, by Kirsten Ralov, *introduction by Walter Terry*

I Was There, by Walter Terry, *compiled and edited by Andrew Wentink, introduction by Anna Kisselgoff*

The Bennington Years: 1934-1942, a chronology and source book, by Sali Ann Kriegsman

The Art and Practice of Ballet Accompanying (in two volumes), by Elizabeth Sawyer Brady

The Ballet Russe (in four volumes), edited by George Jackson

Imperial Dancer, a biography of Felia Doubrovska, by Victoria Huckenpahler

Antony Tudor, a biography, by Fernau Hall

Dancer's Diary, by Dennis Wayne, *introduction by Joanne Woodward*

DANCE OUT
THE ANSWER

Three Pheasant Feathers (China) (Photo: Marcus Blechman, 1946).

DANCE OUT THE ANSWER
an autobiography

La Meri (Russell Meriwether Hughes)

Foreword by John Martin

MARCEL DEKKER, INC.   New York and Basel

Library of Congress Cataloging in Publication Data

Hughes, Russell Meriwether, 1898-
    Dance out the answer.

    (The Dance program ; v. 7)
    Includes index.
    1. Hughes, Russell Meriwether, 1898-
2. Dancers—Biography. 3. Folk dancing. I. Title.
II. Series.
GV1785.H77A33   793.3'092'4 [B]   77-20139
ISBN 0—8247—6633—4

Cover photographs by Marcus Blechman, New York.

MARCEL DEKKER, INC.
270 Madison Avenue, New York, New York 10016

Current printing (last digit):
10 9 8 7 6 5 4 3 2 1

PRINTED IN THE UNITED STATES OF AMERICA

To the perceptive and prolific writer on dance

Walter Terry

with admiration and affection

tell him there is measure in everything
and so dance out the answer

William Shakespeare

Foreword

La Meri and I have something in common besides dancing: we both happen to have been born in Louisville. We had no knowledge of this, however, until neither of us had lived there for a long time.

Her family took her off to Texas at an early age, while it was still the largest state in the union. There were no petroleum millionaires there then, and no astronauts; only a lot of space (which is the natural milieu of the dancer), a lot of history, many climates, cultures, and cattle, none of which failed to influence her. Including the cattle? Definitely.

Indeed, when she gave her first New York dance recital (far longer ago than any Kentucky gentleman would dream of reminding a Kentucky lady), she distributed as a souvenir program a little sheet of original poems entitled "The Star Roper." I regret to say that I have forgotten their individual content; I do not even remember whether she was dealing with a contest-winning riata-wielder or a noncowbard whose métier was the lassoing of stars. From the nature and scope of her career, it had to be the latter.

How she fared with her lariat among the outer planets I do not know, but certainly she managed to capture the ethereal as well as the physical aspects of most of the heavenly bodies on earth. It was not long before she knew why and how everybody danced—in Africa and India and Spain, in the Near and Far East, in practically every atoll in the South Pacific where there was footroom. And she knew it in her own body, for she danced right along with them all. The only people she seems to have neglected are the Kwakiutls, and you could hardly expect

v

a Texas-bred Kentuckian to be drawn to the climate of the Far
North. (Or did I perhaps miss her Kwakiutl recital?)

Her research (a chilling word for such impassioned a calling)
was thoroughly authentic (another frigid term, which simply
means genuine); but she obviously had to resort to artistry in
order to present it to spectators. After all, many of the dances
of the East last all night. In the exercise of such artistry, she
was fortunately equipped with not only a sense of selectivity but
also a sense of humor—the gentle kind that is so much a part of
the charm of Kentucky women. Not that she was concerned in
any degree with making jokes; but simply that she was able to
play with the material she knew so well in order to clarify its
character. I shall never forget her staging and dancing of the
second act of *Swan Lake*, to the Tchaikovsky music, in the
style of Bharata Natya. It was not in the least funny; it simply
made clear to Western minds the values of an important Hindu
dance style.

One final point has to do with her professional name. She
was christened Russell Meriwether Hughes, patently for family
reasons. Certainly, they could not have called her that, but
what they did call her among themselves is not on the record.
Nevertheless, one thing is definite: when she got around to
studying native dances in Mexico and finally made her professional debut in a tour that started in San Antonio and worked
its way south of the border, there were only two syllables of her
long name that were conceivably pronounceable down there.
Ergo—La Meri. This may have been, indeed, the first time she
danced out the answer.

John Martin

Acknowledgments

I wish to thank Carolyn Stagg for her invaluable editing of the vast welter of material first presented to her in 1965. Yet I would never have had the courage to face the task again if it had not been for the friendly nagging of my good friend Cary. And while I was bogged down in the whole thing all else would have fallen apart save for the serene presence of Osceoloa Harris. I also owe thanks to Nancy Brown who typed up the cut-and-pasted-and-stapled (and misspelled) pages as they came off my own typewriter.

La Meri

Contents

Illustrations

Other Works by the Author

Dance As an Art-Form, Principles of the Dance-Art
Gesture Language of the Hindu Dance (*two editions*)
Basic Elements of Dance Composition
Spanish Dancing (*two editions*)
Total Education in Ethnic Dance

DANCE OUT
THE ANSWER

The First Twenty-two Years

This is the chronicle of five decades of devotion to dance . . . how I got there, what I did there, and how I could not give it up. There was a lot of hard work, glamour, and a good deal of unpremeditated comedy. There was also some heartbreak, but I have touched lightly on this, for everyone must face sorrows and, by and large, life has been very good to me.

I was born on Friday, May 13, 1898, in an elegant "mauve decade" house in Louisville, Kentucky, and christened Russell Meriwether Hughes after my father. My mother, Lily Allen, was a woman of great beauty with a strong streak of Scottish moral stubbornness. To my father hard work was a joyful challenge and laughter a way of life. My only sister, Lilian, was always my best friend.

The Hughes family was peripatetic, and even as a babe in arms I was traveling from Kentucky to the Virginia mountains to Florida to New York and, best of all, to Texas. I still love the sound of a train whistle, for those coal-run monsters that belched cinders over one all day and all night were the open sesame to new worlds.

I was still on the sunny side of four years when the family moved to San Antonio, Texas, where Pappy was building a branch of his business. Lil and I fell in love immediately with the town, which was not the thruway-girdled city it is today, but a cowboy's town with one paved street and the Mexican army's barracks still standing on Houston Street. Mother, I am sure, thought it the jumping-off place of creation, and for a few years we "commuted" back to Louisville to attend school. But before I was in high school we had moved permanently to San

1

Antonio, and if I ever enter heaven, I shall not feel a deeper
thrill than I experienced when the sleeper from New Orleans was
shunted off in the San Antonio dawn and I lay, unsleeping in
my berth, and sniffed that marvelous clear air of my own adolescent paradise.

I believe the keynote of my life has been energetic drive.
From the first I did everything that came to hand with a passion
to do it well. At six years I began violin lessons and studied for
eight years. In high school I studied voice, dramatic art, painting . . . and by then was playing in the local symphony orchestra. At twelve I started dancing lessons with the local Cechetti-
trained ballet teacher, and a few years after that my verses began
to appear in the local papers.

On the "fun" side I rode horseback, swam and played tennis,
and when I was thirteen, Daddy, always a motorcar buff, gave
me my own car. (In those days there was no age limit for drivers, and anyone could get a license for thirty-five cents.) About
that time I also discovered boys, and weekends and holidays
were nightly filled with dances.

My parents were enthusiastic theatergoers, and I was not slow
to catch the fever. I vaguely remember Loie Fuller's flowing
scarves and Lillian Russell's enchanting smile, and the first production of *The Wizard of Oz* with David Montgomery and Lewis
Stone is very clear in my memory. Then, in the winter of 1912,
Anna Pavlova came to San Antonio's Grand Opera House for a single magical performance. Her vehicle was *The Magic Flute,* in
which her first entrance was purely pantomimic. I have to confess
that my first glimpse of her was a letdown. "Norme Talmadge is
much prettier," I told myself traitorously.

But then Madame Pavlova came out on the stage and danced.
Everything else faded away. Young as I was, I could feel in the
marrow of my bones a beauty of movement that the world has
yet to see surpassed.

It was several days before I fully grapsed that what I had seen
was dance and that via *glisé, coupé, jeté,* I might aspire to it, perhaps even attain it.

Two months from the time I entered Miss Moore's ballet

classes she staged a dance recital and I was to make a brief appearance in the *Dance of the Hours.* Many of my closest friends were soloists; one of them was even to dance on her toes! I was the rotund but starry-eyed youngster in the last row at the darkest moment, the chorus of "Night." This did not disturb me; in fact, I was blissfully unaware of any implication. I was too enchanted with my dark purple tunic and my long black tights.

I have never made an appearance more perfect than that one! The jammed dressing rooms were for me the very essence of glamour. The stage seemed gigantic, the lights fantastic, the audience miraculously perceptive, giving its thunderous applause. Unlike the majority of mothers, my own forbore to station herself backstage to fuss over me, so I was free to drink in rapturously the wonder of it all.

When it was all over, Pappy was at the stage door to take me home. As we drove through the magical shadowy streets, Pappy murmured, "Who'd have thought that at my time of life I'd be going home with a chorus girl!" It was his incomparable knack for turning heavy emotion into airy joking. But it was something more; it was my accolade, bowing me into the company of professionals. My cup overflowed. Happy tears rolled down my fat, rouged cheeks.

A few months later the annual celebration of the Fiesta of San Jacinto was in preparation, and one night of the week's gaiety was given over to a performance by San Antonio's amateur dancers. A blond beauty named Margaret was given the role of the Little Princess to dance, and I was one of a covey of tunic-clad handmaidens escorting her.

After the very last rehearsal the director announced that owing to the demand for tickets, there would be two performances, matinee and evening. This displeased Margaret's mother, who rose up to counter majestically that *her* daughter would not be appearing at the matinee performance since it was absolutely essential for her to rest and have her hair curled for the evening performance.

Miss Moore was thunderstruck. At her wits' end she turned to the assembled wide-eyed youngsters and whimpered, "Oh, dear, is there *any* little girl here who can dance the role of the Little Princess without a rehearsal?"

"I can," I heard myself pipe up calmly.

Mother sat up half the night sewing spangles and roses on my handmaiden costume. And there, at the matinee, was fat little Dickie Hughes, translated into a beautiful princess. Oddly enough, I have no memory of the effect it had, either on the audience or on the momentary star. Terpsichore, the witch, must have chuckled mightily, though, having gained a "hand-maiden" she would never again lose!

Pappy's health was failing frighteningly. Often nowadays I observed him quiet and serious; never did he raise his voice or al-low his nerves to betray him into losing his temper. I think he must have felt a despairing aloneness toward the end, but always for his family he had laughter, love, and endless patience. Never was he too busy to draw a funny picture, tell a funny story, or fashion a nonsense song for his children.

On the night of May 15, 1914, my pardner, tired from a life-time of grueling work and old before his time, left us forever. I do not remember Pappy's face when he went to his last rest, only how stiff his crossed hands were, those wonderful, pliable square hands that could coax the heart out of a violin or a child.

The change in Mother was immediate and marked. In a mat-ter of months she aged terribly. Her glorious auburn hair was streaked with white, and instead of drooping wistfully her mouth tightened in nervous anxiety. In her own heart her life had ended, but she threw herself unconditionally into the task of sole parent, meeting it brilliantly. For the moment income was adequate for our support. But with war on the horizon, for how long? So we "made do." I personally felt no pinch, being perfectly happy with my pretty homemade dresses, our ancient car, and Mother's can-opener cookery. For a long time I have known that the experience was good for me. Providentially, it taught me to put material comforts in second place and not to panic over financial upheavals, which, believe me, I was to learn to expect later in theater life as at least every-other-day occurrences.

Mother, Pappy, and Lilian, 1896.

April 1, 1915, was an important date for me, for the Denishawn Company danced in San Antonio. Seated in the Opera
House, I remembered somewhat smugly that in two weeks I
would be dancing on that same stage.

Tall, exquisite Miss Ruth, in her *Dance of the Five Senses,*
stepped from her golden throne straight into the very heart of
my being. It goes without saying that Mr. Shawn—Bacchus in a
tiger skin!—was surely the answer to a young maid's dream.

This utterly glamorous introduction to the East set me off on
a spree of reading everything I could lay hands on pertaining to
the subject—poetry, travel, history, even philosophy. I established an all-girl club, which I called The Alhambra of Tooba,
and sternly required all members to read my accumulated books.
We wore "Oriental" costumes and, as could be predicted, I conducted classes in "Oriental" dancing. In my abysmal ignorance
"Oriental" was all of a piece, the Orient being a big romantic
domain of harems, flying carpets, and yogis; and I casually mixed
Moorish, Indian, Turkish, Armenian and what-have-you to suit
the requirements of the moment.

On a very different stage, before a very different audience, I
was to see another great dance genius of the day.

With a good deal of finagling I persuaded Mother to let me go
with my current swain to the little theater down in the Mexican
quarter. Small, poorly placed, it nevertheless presented some of
the best professionals, well known in the top theaters of Mexico
City. A Spanish dancer was performing there and some instinct
told me not to miss her.

A *tonadillera,* tall, green-eyed, utterly charming, she whistled
better than she sang, but she could have done neither and still
would have been a huge success, for her castanets spoke for her.
She was billed as La Argentina, and I saw her for twenty-five
cents.

At my next lesson with Miss Moore I said I must be taught
Spanish dancing. Miss Moore was delighted to agree. She had
studied in Spain and played castanets. "I will teach you a Spanish dance you can do for the Fiesta Queen at her coronation,"
she cried excitedly. "And I myself will play castanets for you

I begin to dance, 1910.

from the wings, for you cannot possibly learn these also in three weeks."

She was so right! I know now that if a dancer can dance with castanets after six months of unbroken labor, she is nothing less than a dedicated genius. But I did not know this then. In blissful ignorance I found a pair of castanets somewhere, put a Waldteufel waltz on the victrola, and for ten days made everyone's life a misery with my clatter.

On the night of the coronation I did indeed appear; wrapped in Grandma Lucy's ivory shawl, a high comb and a rose in my hair, I danced a fandango, insisting even on plonking my own castanets.

There are, I learned, ways of carrying off inexpert dancing. Many attributes not acquired in the classroom will hold an audience. They have to do with character and personality in the dancer and stem from an individual and great love for the theater. A feeling of being personally at home on the stage can cause the very curtains to come to life. Then there is that subconscious bond of unity with an audience that can translate a performance into a lovers' dialogue, exchanged by two lovers finding themselves miraculously alone together in time and space. I have felt myself an alien for half my life. But never, *never* on a stage! The black velvet draperies and gray floorcloth that constituted the setting for my career were my home. Here, and only here, do I come to feel supremely comfortable, supremely happy—for always there is my "lover" facing me just across the footlights.

The same week in which I performed my fandango I appeared in the Fiesta Fete as the leading "male" dancer in Miss Moore's ballet *Zingara*. To my good friend Grace as the gypsy girl and beautiful Margaret as the Princess I played the Prince.

This *Zingara* deal boiled with all sorts of eddies. In herself, Margaret was a wonderfully sweet girl. It was her mother who harbored the ideas.

In the second scene of the ballet the Prince and Princess were to ride onstage on a horse. A beautiful pure-white circus horse,

Arabia, had been engaged. Being an old trouper, he needed no rehearsal.

The night of the show Arabia arrived with his trainer, who stated without delay that the horse would not carry two people. Into the dispute leaped Margaret's mother. Very well, then, Margaret would ride and the Prince would walk.

It was not a big point to me. "All right," said I. "Let's get on with it." But I reckoned without my sister. Lilian sprang from the wings, announcing hotly, "Dickie will *not* enter walking while Margaret rides."

Irresistible force meeting immovable body—for several aeons the curtain was held. Finally, our entrance. Prince, Princess, and Arabia, *all* walking. "That's my sister, Lilian," I muttered to myself.

In a sea of organdy, roses, and parties I graduated from Mulhollands High School. I knew myself to be a woman grown, ready to put away childish things. I was bursting at the seams to "get at it." Only . . . to get at what? Therein lay my problem.

In the fall of 1916 I enrolled at the College of Industrial Arts in Denton, Texas. This highly respected institution is now the State Teachers College and has graduated many teachers of modern dance. But in 1916 the "Dance Department" was run by my friend Grace and myself. The department functioned only in recreation hours and strictly on a special-permission-from-higher-authorities basis. The wearing of gym clothes was rigidly decreed—middy blouses, heavy knee-length bloomers, long cotton stockings, gym shoes. But we liked it in spite of all the taboos. And although I played in the school orchestra, sang a small solo in the cantata, and swashbuckled my way through the title role of *David Garrick* in the drama class production, I was happiest in my role of Pan in the spring festival.

In this outdoor pageant, as Pan I sat on a very uncomfortable tree stump, tootling on a paper pipe. When the flutist in the orchestra finished "our" solo, it became my duty to scramble from my perch and leap à la Nijinsky into Spring's bower to

awaken her to life. Having thus "motivated" the hundred or so
other participants into action, I returned to my pipe and tree
stump for the duration.

Thrice during the school year the student body, in full uniform, was allowed to leave Denton. Once we went to Dallas to
the state fair. Another time we went to see Geraldine Farrar in
Carmen, an experience that made me immediately into a "Gerry
Flapper." Once a few of us signed up to go to Fort Worth to
see the Ballets Russes. This was the first tour of the Diaghilev
company.

The stars were Nijinsky, Karsavina and Lydia Lopoukhova.
The program included *L'Après-Midi d'un Faune, Schéhérazade,
Le Carnaval,* and *Le Spectre de la Rose.* Intellectually the whole
thing was way over my head, of course, but the emotional impact was so tremendous that the evening proved too much for
me. On the way back to school I became deathly sick and remained ill for several days. I sometimes feel that destiny should
be a bit more leisurely about portioning out such soul-shaking
events to those so totally unprepared for them as I was at that
juncture.

At the close of school in the spring my roommate invited me
to visit her father's ranch in south Texas. The TV Ranch (nothing to do with today's channels and electronics) was not one of
those feudal jobs that dot Texas, taking up so much of her
acreage, but an old-timer—comfortable, unpretentious, run along
old-time lines. Hot and dusty in the summer months, it stretched
for many barren miles from the low, rambling, breeze-swept,
gray frame ranch house. Corrals, bunkhouses, windmill, and silo
clustered companionably around the main house; far away were
the lonesome cabins and corrals of the line camps.

Sunrises and sunsets were pageants of glory. Mockingbirds
sang all night under the brilliant summer moon. Here was the
Texas I had loved, yet scarcely known.

For long hours at a time I hung around the cowboys, swap-
ping yarns while they squatted on their heels in the shadow of
the bunkhouse. Endlessly we rode across the plains, swam in the
irrigation tank, and savored goat barbecue at special parties. But

my crowning moments came when I was invited to join the cowboys at a line camp to cut out sixty head for sale to a neighboring ranchman.

There was no branch water at the camp, so we drank canned
pineapple juice with our goat and beans, served from the chuck
wagon. And how one can eat—and sleep—after following a herd
of bawling cattle forty dusty miles! Even the sight of tomorrow's
dinner, blatting plaintively beside the wagonwheel, could not
turn my appetite.

When the cattle were all herded into a hollow of the plains,
the tricky business of cutting out the sixty selected steers would
begin. I had been warned that I must work or walk and was
given a top horse that knew more about cattle than I will ever
find out.

The top hands rode into the midst of the milling animals to
cut out those selected by the buyer, who sat his horse on a rise
of ground a little apart. I was one of the riders whose duty it
was to keep the herd together, bringing back any recalcitrants
that made a sudden dash for liberty. Since my cow pony knew
his business, when a walleyed steer jumped the herd and headed
for the brush, I found myself a willing and exhilarated passenger
on a long chase through tearing mesquite thickets. All credit to
my pony that we never lost an animal!

I was very proud of the long, bloody gouge in my thigh, dealt
out to me by a protruding brush limb. But then, people are
divided into two kinds—performers and audience—those who do
and those who watch. Pappy's daughter was never cut out to sit
on the sidelines; body and soul alike can get pretty lacerated
when one is in there, getting things done.

On the ranch I discovered the cowboy who was to become
the means of my coping with Euterpe, who until now had proven
somewhat indifferent to my Oriental flights. Under my typing
fingers Silver Cy and Whiskey Pete came to life. Pages flew,
bristling with valorous horses, cattle, six-guns, and fight-provok-
ing senoritas. At last I was on my way, albeit slowly. Now and
then an acceptance actually broke the monotony of rejection
slips in my mail.

World War I—"the war to end all wars!"—was now on in
earnest. The normal come-aliveness of San Antonio in fall was
augmented by an accelerating colorful activity, revolving around
the military. Seven wartime camps had sprung up for the troops,
and the city teemed with them. Each camp bulged with lonely,
uprooted young men. Any female who was even approximately
presentable and could dance had a waiting list of dates like the
tail of a kite. There were simply not enough hours in the day,
not enough days in the week! Sunday-afternoon open house
was reestablished at our house, and Lilian and I, at last for social
purposes the same age, spun in a vortex of khaki-clad young
stalwarts, while in a corner of the parlor our chaperone, Mother,
lent a reassuring ear to the homesick, whose sharp need was
someone motherly to talk to.

There was a spreading mania for patriotic activity. Biweekly
the girls made excursions to the "Y" huts to give little shows
for the boys; we were waitresses for a day at free dinners; we
were name-tagged "taxi dancers" at free dances. In the daytime
we rolled miles of bandages, scraped tons of lint, and no girl was
properly dressed to go out without a knitting bag. We started
on scarves and worked our way up through sweaters to socks, as
many a bunion-cursed doughboy found reason to remember.

Weekly I fell in and out of love with young men from all over
the country and from a few distant countries as well. I danced
miles and miles with soldiers and for soldiers, and when entertainment programs were insufficient, as they often were, I could
be depended upon to dash forth, carrying the biggest Tri-color
this side of France, to sing "La Marseillaise" in a willing but
wobbly soprano. They were very fine days for me. Looking
very young and reasonably pretty, in a plump sort of way, I
found a readymade audience for whatever I agreed—nay, leaped—
to do, from dancing on point in a stars-and-stripes tutu to de-
claiming humorous cowboy verse.

Into the midst of our teeming, laughing town suddenly strode
the specter of Spanish influenza. I believe it was recorded as
the worst plague ever to decimate the United States. In the

camps soldiers dropped at their work like flies. All places of
amusement were closed; it was forbidden for more than five persons to congregate in private homes. Storehouses and auto sales-
rooms were cleared out to receive towering stacks of coffins,
both occupied and empty. Superannuated doctors were called
from retirement by hysterical patients who could not be made
to believe that these experienced men of medicine were at a
tragic loss as to how to combat this roaring enemy.

Lilian and I were among the earlier victims of the flu. After a
glamorous Thanksgiving party at which, in a brand-new dress of
black velvet, I had cut quite a swath, I went to bed to dream of
the handsome new lieutenant who had dated me for the morrow.
But it would be a month before I left my bed again. With me
ill in one room and Lilian in another, Mother kept herself going
frantically on endless headache pills and the courage of total
desperation. The harassed old doctor who finally squeezed in
time to visit us said to Mother, "I can try to save your older
daughter, madam; the young one will die no matter what I do,
and you must understand that I cannot take time from the pos-
sible-to-save to give to the already lost." Since I was not conscious enough to know of this iron pronouncement, I did not
say to anyone in so many words that I had no intention of dying. But then, Mother was not of the stuff that gives up either.

One night in late autumn we were all awakened abruptly by a
sound that was a distant, bewildering sort of roar, punctuated by
gunshots. We sat up in our beds, noticing that over toward the
main part of town the sky had a strange pink glare. In a kind
of panic we started to jabber, but then, suddenly, some atavistic
radar told us . . .

"The war's over!" Lilian screeched. "It's armistice!" She and
I began scrambling our way into robes and slippers.

"And where do you think you're going?" Mother asked
reprovingly.

"Why, to town, of course."

"Nothing of the kind," she said. "Get straight back into your
beds. Girls . . . in the streets . . . on such a night! You must
be crazy!"

"Everybody should be crazy on a night when the war's over!"
I said, well knowing I was in a losing battle.

Lilian said, "But, Mother, you don't understand. The war's
over. This is the sort of event that comes only once in a life-
time. It'd be wrong for us not to see it . . . wrong . . . wrong . . ."

"Back into your beds," Mother said bleakly.

Of course she was right. It wouldn't have been safe for us,
but how could we have known it then? Indeed, I didn't really
know it until thirty years later when I traipsed the whole
screaming length of Broadway in New York City from 59th
Street to Eighth Street, madly celebrating a mad V-E Day.

But on that November 11, 1918, obediently I returned to bed,
if not to sleep. Sometime later I crept into the house, into the
quiet of my study, where I sat far past daybreak writing long,
wild letters to the handsome Canadian, the charming Frenchman,
the distinguished Britisher . . . and to any and every other soldier
I could recall even faintly.

When the morning of November 12 bloomed over a strangely
quiet Texas world, I had a small victory of my own to celebrate.
In the mail was a letter from the Gorham Press saying simply
that they were accepting my verses collected under the title of
Mexican Moonlight.

On the privately creative side I succeeded in turning out lyrics
and music for several songs, secular and sacred. I exhibited two
canvases at a Palette-and-Brush Club show, and captured the first
prize for the best one-act play written locally. As I was also
teaching dancing I could tell myself I was achieving forward
movement.

From childhood my parents had impressed upon me that I
could set my hand to whatever I liked so long as I always finished the job, recognizing that the real reward comes in the joy
of accomplishment. I began learning now one very important
by-product of these lessons—namely, the time you saved, so to
speak, from wasting. Instead of standing still after completing a
task, waiting for the recompense to appear, one simply pocketed
the satisfaction and, without a backward glance, turned to something new.

In the spring of 1919 my singing and dramatic teachers decided to present me in recital. My dramatic teacher, Miss
McKeen, arranged for me to give a full evening of readings, interspersed with vocal solos by Lilian. My program was a protean
affair of poems both dramatic and comic and one full act of *The
Taming of the Shrew.*

Five days later my voice teacher, Mrs. Baggett, presented me
in a song recital. This time Lilian assisted with violin solos.
Dressed as nearly like Geraldine Farrar as I could manage, I gave
out with such modest works as the "Habañera" from *Carmen,*
"Un bel di" from *Madame Butterfly,* and Handel's "Jubal's
Lyre." I had a wonderful time and did not worry about the
comfort of my hearers.

Mother was impressed by my dogged efforts to place my little
poems and took to looking with favor on a literary career if I
wanted it. She consulted with Miss Decker, my high school
teacher of English literature, and was persuaded that the best, if
not the only, place where I might get expert guidance in the art
of versification was Columbia University.

This would be expensive and require a good deal of arranging,
but Mother's Scotch streak was not atrophied. Since Daddy's
death she had been amazingly clever at budgeting. She had managed to handle her $100 per month "salary" as president of
R. M. Hughes & Co. so that a nest egg of hard-pinched dollars
was laid by for just such an eventuality as this.

In a seventh-heaven daze I prepared to set off. We took advantage of the annual company-paid trip to Louisville to get that
far. After the directors' meeting Lilian returned to San Antonio
while Mother and I pressed on to New York.

We went straight up to the vicinity of the university to find a
place for me to live. My first sight of Broadway, even in the
nontheatrical 116th Street section, was a dazzling thrill.

Christmas of 1920 was miraculous. All decked out in evening
clothes, my escort and I went down to the theater section of
Broadway. Between 43rd and 51st Streets some forty-odd
theaters lifted lighted facades into the night. No garish neons,
but electric globes in many colors and moving patterns

announced the glamour names: the *Ziegfeld Follies,* the *Carroll Vanities,* Al Jolson, Ed Wynn, Mae West, Ann Pennington, Irene Bordoni. A light snow was falling and dulled the sound of taxi and limousine debouching elegantly dressed passengers at the wide, brilliant theater entrances.

We went to *The Greenwich Village Follies,* where I saw a slim, serious girl perform a sort of Javanese dance. Her name, the program said, was Martha Graham. She fascinated me completely by doing some extraordinarily supple waist turns from the floor.

After the show we went on to a nightclub to see Gilda Gray do her famous shimmy dance in a pink velvet evening gown, her short blond curls bobbing.

"Hail and farewell, Broadway!" Things happened, the money gave out, and we returned to San Antonio with little to show for my "literary career" save the inclusion of one small poem in an *Anthology of Dance Poems* published by Knopf.

San Antonio Carousel
and New York Show Biz

Life back in San Antonio became for me like riding some carousel, trying to catch a hold first on one, then another of the varicolored horses flashing by, scarlet-painted nostrils flaring, lacquered manes flying to the endless accompaniment of piercing music. One leaped from ground to steed, any steed, and leaned far out to snatch the prize ring. I did not pick one horse and stay with it. I chose and discarded and chose again, as though always with a new mount I would surely capture the prize.

Of all I tried the silliest was the pink horse of the social whirl. On this giddy nag I spun the party round. Always this pink horse seemed to have been hollowed out by termites, for most of my high school friends were married, and from the seniority of my two or three years I found the "younger generation" very boring.

I discarded the pink horse for the red horse of sports—shooting, swimming, tennis, but mostly riding. I got up at six in the morning to head for the army post and the ladies' riding class. After the deep stock saddles to which I was accustomed, an English saddle seemed like trying to ride a billiard ball; but I began learning to control a horse with my knees and the double bridle. Then came the hurdles. The class grew noticeably smaller. We "graduated" to cross-country riding. A horse following the tail of the horse ahead in a closed ring is a horse on a merry-go-round. A horse in open country is another thing altogether. Over four-foot obstacles that do not, like the bars of an indoor ring, give to the brush of a careless hoof . . . down precipitous slides and up again . . . splashing gallops through rocky streams . . . dismounts in fields and remounts, on a horse already jittery from racing . . . wheeling constantly away from equally nervous rider. Finally, Major Jones pronounced us accredited riders, though a good bit of doubt remained in the minds of most of us.

It is a tradition that you are not really a rider till you have been thrown seven times; why seven precisely, I don't know. Once I was asked to ride in a quarter-mile flat race. "We'll get a horse for you," said the colonel's wife. On the whole it was pretty sporting of her inasmuch as recently I had made a spectacle of myself. A reserve officer, riding a McClellan saddle in a paper chase, had caught his covered stirrup in my spur when we crowded on the hurdle. I went down. My mount galloped away with the field; I rolled wildly under the hurdle, staring fascinated and with only inches to spare at the hooves of fifty horses flying over my head, throwing their dust in my face.

I was so frightened by the prospect of the flat race that I decided to tell Mother I would telephone to say I was unable to ride in the event. Mother was deathly afraid of horses herself, so I felt sure she would be all sympathy and approval. But I should have known. With my mother there were things stronger than fear.

"You have agreed to ride and you must do so," she said, fixing me with a cold blue eye. "Here, take a spoonful of my nerve tonic, but promise you'll never touch it without permission."

Having gulped the tonic, I rode shakily out to the race course, Mother straight-backed beside me.

The horse they had unearthed for me was a complete stranger not only to me but evidently to the idea of racing. This heavy-set bay, responding after a fashion to the contradictory name Getaway, regarded me with a chilly eye.

I saw that I was not the only jittery rider. The whole lot looked downright wan. None of us had ever ridden a flat race before. We were briefed on the basic etiquette. No cutting under on the rail. Winner not to leave the track after the race. And so on. I was in such a droop by now that I hardly grasped anything.

On the way to the post Getaway and I worked up quite a mutual hate. The gun went off, the ribbon flew up, I became merely an unwilling passenger. Getaway, sourly declining to live up to his name, bunched in with the field, well behind the leaders. At some point amid the dust and thunder I became aware that someone had cut under to the rail on the turn. It should not have made me mad, for I could have been pretty sure the lady didn't even know she'd done it. But make me mad it did.

By now we were coming down the stretch. To Getaway's infinite and disgusted surprise I went suddenly to whip and spur, unorthodoxly adding a stream of imprecations. We passed the field; we edged up on the beautifully handled leader and a dappled gray running second. It looked as though the best I could manage would be third place, when suddenly the gray stumbled and fell. Having no idea how, we hurdled the heap and came in a screaming second, both of us filthy with the dust we'd taken.

Happy? I was hysterical. God only knew what agonies of fear Mother was going through in the stands. I rushed to her.

"That was very good," she remarked. "Go and wash your face."

The pale horse on my carousel was music. I mounted up Sunday mornings for church choir and on other, singularly uninspiring occasions. This was a horse devoid of drama, certainly of humor.

I was asked to play violin for the reunion of Confederate Veterans. The gentle old men, reminiscing quietly among themselves, were almost childishly anxious to feign an interest in the sassy young miss who came to entertain them. Goodness knows my fiddling skill held all too little promise of amusement for them. But my sense of theater kept me from letting them down.

I picked a composition called, simply, "Fantasy on a Familiar Theme." After a page of cadenza, to which my audience listened respectfully, I began the simple theme, which developed through three pages of violinistic fireworks. To my sorrow I played this rather poorly, but it turned out not to matter at all, for the melodic line proved to be "Dixie." No sooner were the first measures identifiable than my ancient listeners let out one long

Rebel yell, which they kept going to the end. When it was over, we were all thoroughly exhausted, but my audience had a new lease on life. As far as they were concerned, the sassy young miss was the greatest violinist extant.

It should have struck joy to me. In a way it was delightfully funny. Actually, I nearly wept, for I was brushing the edge of that responsibility that must be the constant concern and burden of anyone aspiring to be a true artist—the responsibility that is the power to awaken dormant emotions.

One of the smaller San Antonio movie houses, the Rialto, scheduled a film about an opera singer. Indicated in the script of this silent film was a theme song, "Ben Bolt." I was engaged to sing the song for the run of the film—one afternoon and two evenings.

A pianist provided an ad lib accompaniment from the pit; sitting by the piano, I quivered and quavered my way through the tale of Ben's Alice. At the end of the run I received $25. In itself it was a minor incident, but since it was my first "professional" engagement, this round on the pale horse emboldened me.

Shortly, the Rialto announced a beauty contest to find the new "Ince Girl." The theater manager suggested that I enter, and I made bold to try another carousel steed, this time a dappled gray, representing for me the movies.

Happily the contest specifications included talent and legs as well as face. I was one of the two winners, and presently I was an entranced member of a small movie company shooting westerns in and around San Antonio. As the villain's sister I galloped around, leading the sheriff on wild-goose chases and becoming involved in cattle stampedes, taking a good deal of rough treatment in the "shack set"; that is, I did when I could be found; a good part of the time I spent either riding about on my own or lending an ear to the tall—very tall—tales of cowpoke extras in the company.

My best pal was called—what else—Shorty. A stocky individual with a face like an Irish potato, he had, as far as anyone knew, no surname. Among other things, Shorty was flattering to me,

being full of respectful interest in my city ways. In spite of the
fact that prohibition had driven him to tippling rather staggering
quantities of horse linament, he was a sensitive and gentle man
who took a good deal of trouble over Mother's comfort whenever she visited me on location. In a sense I think he felt he
owed it to her for the figure I cut. The first time he saw me in
leather skirt and 10-gallon hat he spat admiringly, declaring for
all to hear, "If yew knowed how good yew look in them duds,
yew'd never wear no diff'rent!" Our putteed director was less
enthusiastic; behind his megaphone he would often declare
meaningfully that I'd be wonderful—in comedy. Notwithstanding,
some years later, when I chanced to go into a small movie
theater on upper Broadway in New York to see a Douglas Fair-
banks feature, my eyes popped when the second feature came
on. It was a horse opera, and it was good to see the familiar
faces of my companions in the *Big Bend Company* and watch us
shoot our way through a few reels.

The dark horse on my carousel was the dance. I rode this
one increasingly often and, of them all, with the most élan. War
Department entertainment units actually hired me to dance,
billing me as a star "resting after an arduous season on the silver
screen." The Austin American Legion "imported" me for some
Spanish dances, auctioning off the numbers on my dance card at
the ball that followed. I was engaged to dance at the Cotton Palace in Waco, and my appearance before the court of this "queen"
was such that I received a "royal command" to dance for San
Antonio's "queen" of the Court of Birds.

For this occasion I made a dance titled *The White Peacock,*
inspired by photographs of Gertrude Hoffman in a dance of the
same name. For music I chose Delibes's *Passepied,* and I made
the movements actually peacocky. The number, which remained
in my repertory for many years, ultimately evolved into an interpretation of Griffes's beautiful *White Peacock* composition,
which I danced in a costume made especially in Paris. It was
welcomed by audiences on five continents; a bemused reviewer
in Australia wrote, "We much prefer La Meri's arrogant peacock
to Pavlova's self-pitying Swan."

As easy as I found my dark horse to ride in small, familiar rings, my eye kept straying to that pinto just over there. Her name was Euterpe.

The publication of *Mexican Moonlight* had projected me into the (very lesser) ranks of the professionals. The next year Cornhill published another collection, titled *Poems of the Plains.* Since all my material was western and my name was Russell Meriwether Hughes, I was inevitably taken for a man, and I carried on a mild personal correspondence with several fellow rhymesters under that misconception.

Indeed, the pinto mustang carried me well until I traduced her. I fell in love again. Putting aside my Stetson for the crown of roses with many thorns, I took to singing of love, preferably unrequited. With celerity the lyric world that had welcomed Mr. Hughes became bored with this mauve-minded poetess. In terms of further publication the pinto mustang threw me off with gusto and galloped off to Parnassus in search of a disciple who would be more dedicated.

For a couple of years this carousel-hopping continued. There was a round on the dark horse in a "tour" I booked down the Rio Grande valley. On the pinto I enrolled at Our Lady of the Lake College for courses in history and literature. There were minor rounds on the red horse and even the pink one. Like a half-broken colt I just couldn't seem to understand the directions life was trying to give me. Then Terpsichore, wearying of my obtuseness, chivvied me into position.

Talking pictures were still a Hollywood mixture of day-dreaming and prophecy. All over the country certain theaters were becoming "presentation houses" with a stage prologue to the still silent films a sine qua non. From time to time I had appeared in some of these. Then, early in 1924, Mme. Phillippini, wife of the orchestra conductor and presentation director at the Empire Theatre, made a contract with me for eight straight weeks. The prologues took in a wide range of material—dancing, singing, even acting. Four shows a day, five on Saturdays and Sundays, plus my studies kept me pretty busy. One week I would be in my Pola Negri aspect, doing a Spanish dance; the next I would be an "emoting" Alice Terry, complete with blond wig. Or I would be doing an Oriental number for *The Thief of Bagdad.*

The eighth week Mme. Phillippini booked in a baritone named MacDonald. To his singing of "Flower from an Old Bouquet" I performed a dance on point. The production went over so well that it was held for a second week. Then Mr. MacDonald persuaded me to go with him for a run at the cinema palace in New Orleans. Mother and I packed our suitcases for a couple of weeks there.

Mr. MacDonald said he had booked the act into Atlanta. It wasn't far, so we went there too. One town led to another. By late spring we had worked our way north to New York.

This time I was really imprisoned. I informed Mother then, definitely, I was going into the theater.

Our financial situation was, as usual, not bright. The fact was, Mother couldn't afford to stay in New York with me. She sat down and, after a long stint of figuring, came up with the decision that I could stay in New York—*if* I could make it on $20 a week.

Rapid calculation, liberally seasoned with wishful thinking, convinced me. David, Lilian's handsome lieutenant husband, was now stationed at West Point. He offered me a birthday gift of a commutation ticket; I could go to the Point for weekends, thereby enabling me to count on free food for three days a week. Calculating $8 a week for a room and $1 a day for food four days a week, I would be left with $8 for dancing lessons and subway travel. Why, this was a patrimony.

I did my best to get started that summer. I studied ballet with Tarasoff, tap at Chorus Equity, and, now and then, Spanish with Arriaza and Ortega.

Bookings were slow, summer theaters all but unknown. Also, I didn't really know how to look for work, something of an art in itself. Still feeling the alien in an unfamiliar land, I admired the professionals in my dancing classes without ever being able to get on enough of a footing with them to learn from them how to go about getting a job.

In terms of morale, the weekends at West Point kept me going. All those handsome young men! All those brass buttons! The hops, the rides along mountain trails, the Sunday morning chapels . . . and "the long, gray line." I would not have missed it for anything!

In spite of my best efforts, the theater still eluded me. Mother, having saved up a small nest egg, joined me in New York. We settled down in a theatrical hotel just off Broadway. I knew nobody, had no real connections whatever. Ignorantly optimistic once more, with no idea what I was getting into, I copied addresses out of the classified pages and began making the rounds. The theatrical caste system was unknown to me and I was impartially brash, entering a Shubert office as readily as that of a third-rate vaudeville booker. Everywhere I registered as "dancer, singer, actress, violinist," feeling that if I threw out enough lines, something was bound to come back on at least one hook.

I almost got a job in the road company of *White Cargo* . . . almost. I almost got into Earl Carroll's *Vanities* . . . almost. I almost got "chorus and specialty" with the *Ziegfeld Follies* . . . almost. I did get a job in burlesque to do a strip tease with a fiddle instead of a fan, but was warned off in time.

I almost got into a dramatic stock company. At least I had learned by this time that the one thing one does *not* say is that one has had no professional experience. So they asked me where I had worked in stock, and I named the stock company that had played San Antonio some years in the past.

"That's funny," brooded the director. "I was directing that company and I don't seem to place you."

This brought me up so short that I veered over to posing for a while as an English professional. I got my deserts. Auditioning for a vaudeville act, I said that my experience had been in England; of course it turned out that the director was English! "Oh, what a tangled web we weave . . ." Well, how under the sun do you get around it? If you have no experience, you can't get work to get experience!

I did get a job, and a strange one it was! I was hired to play castanets in the wings for a Spanish dancer who was starred in a vaudeville act. She was very beautiful and danced well, but she was incapable of playing castanets.

Her act didn't last long, but during its run I became friendly with one of the dancers in her troupe, Lita Lopez.

It was Lita who got me into Maria Montero's troupe. At that time Montero was the finest Spanish dancer in America. Tiny, elegant, a true artist, she was a wonderful friend to us all. Between shows she taught me several dances and gave me endless, good, professional advice. With her act I traveled the best of the subway circuit. When we closed, I was far richer in technical experience and knowledge of the stage and its ways.

So things took a turn for the better. With occasional engagements for prologues in outlying movie houses I managed to get together enough money to rent a studio, and there I worked and worked and worked.

However ethereal a dancer may appear onstage, her preparation will have been anything but glamorous. Studio practice is all dust, sweat, tears, and aching muscles. I defy any but that fanatical, brave race known as dancers to survive the two to five hours of daily brute labor that goes into kindling that three-minute spiritual fire that you, out front in the audience, survey and possibly admire from a comfortable seat. If you are one who believes that dancing is an enchantingly easy way to make a living, you could hardly be more mistaken. Physically, it is a very hard way indeed to make a living, and only too often, after the endless hours of preparation, the one thing you haven't done is make a living!

If, however, you are one who loves the dance for itself, then I would say, be a dancer and my blessings on you! To choose it as a career may never bring you fame or money or even the rudimentary comforts. But by its very nature it will at least always insure you plenty of dancing.

Now that I was equipped with a practice studio and an accompanist, my current agent came to observe what I could do. He was an exception in his cynical field, for he was both kind and gentle.

"I like your dancing," he said, "but I know very little about Spanish work, so I'm going to call another agent to come and see you. He is a Spaniard."

It should have put me on my guard. But where I had danced, I had quite often been taken for a native of Spain. Besides, I had reached that stage of trying that recklessly combines animal grit with wishful thinking.

The Spaniard arrived. A romantic apparition! Tall, handsome, gray-haired in a distinguished way, he was elegantly turned out up to and including spats, derby hat and monocle. My eyes bugged out, but I kept my mind fiercely on my work. I tossed off a little comedy song, played a tune on the fiddle, then launched into a Spanish dance.

When I finished, the Spanish gentleman inquired absently, "Have you had any professional experience?"

"Oh, yes," I answered crisply.

"Where?"

I thought fast. More than one lie about experience in both the States and England had previously bitten back. This time I blurted out, "In Mexico." I had never even been there. However, I knew it was conventional for all Latin American capitals to boast national theaters. So I added confidently, "Teatro Nacional in Mexico City."

"Strange," murmured my interrogator, eyeing me, "Teatro Nacional at Mexico City isn't quite completed yet." I hoped that was the hint of a twinkle behind the monocle, but was none too sure.

My self-confidence gave way abruptly. Unnerved, I cried, stamping my foot, "Well, damn it! What d'you expect a girl to say? I know you must have experience in order to be allowed to get any experience . . . and how silly d'you think *that* is? All right, then, you want to know where my experience has been. Well, I'm the amateur pride of San Antonio, Texas, and I've bummed the New York subway circuit . . . so now you know." It was pretty rude; Mother would have been horrified. But I was way beyond caring.

"Well, at least your temperament is Spanish," mused my

tormentor. "Get your clothes on and come over to my office. We will talk about a contract." And out he strolled, leaving me with my mouth hanging open.

Guido Carreras proved to be not Spanish, but an Italian of Spanish descent. And not an agent, but an impresario in the old European tradition. He had worked for the great Busoni, for Pavlova, for Nijinsky. He had come to this country with Eleanora Duse in 1923. He was not at all interested now in booking readymade acts, only in molding artists.

He went to work on me. None of my purported talents were left undissected. The immortal Duse had died in his arms in a Pittsburgh hotel. Since he had listened constantly to her glorious voice, my small abilities as an actress were waved aside. For one thing, I had a southern accent!

On the chance that some capital could be made of my ability with the violin, he had me play for a gifted violinist. The verdict was clear and to the point. "If she had a decent bow," said the violinist, stroking his chin impressively, "and a good violin and worked hard for not less than eight years, I think she might be, well, all right."

I sang for another friend of Carreras's, a singing coach of standing. When I concluded "Un bel di," this gentleman, a Hungarian of gaiety he was, said to me affably, "You have a great deal of artistic understanding . . . and, so far as I can discover, no voice at all."

Having been reared to a standard of honesty, I could give myself no good reason why Carreras should not wash his hands of me forthwith. But he did not, and I was a jelly of gratitude.

He called still another friend. Amalia Molina, the Queen of the Castanets, came to see me dance.

I did the jota.

"Well," said Madame Molina noncommittally, "the dance is Aragonese and the music Navarrese. But, well, let me see something else."

I danced *Mirando a España,* which I had been taught backstage between shows by Maria Montero.

"Of course, her castanets . . ." Madame dismissed my castanets with an impressive wave of the hand. "But," she went on, "yes . . . yes, I have to say she has *something*." I held my breath, waiting for the crusher. "But what is it?"

I gulped. From a Spanish dancer, any Spanish dancer, this amounted to high praise. I was to learn that, on the face of the earth, no artist is so critical as the Spanish dancer of another's performance.

So between Carreras and Amalia Molina the die was cast. I was at the point where I knew I couldn't go on, forever spreading myself thin; I had to get down to one art and concentrate on it.

I threw in my lot with dance. Mr. Carreras informed me that henceforth I would be managed by him.

I was made acquainted at once with the economics of my calling. Being under management, I had to build a costume wardrobe and a repertoire. I saw immediately that if we bought costumes, we couldn't then afford the cost of repertoire. I was not yet skilled enough to make elaborate costumes. So to save money I must make my own repertoire, which I did by trial and error. It is one of the hazards of dance to create and execute five numbers, then keep one and discard four.

As soon as a dance was pronounced usable, Mother made a costume on a rented sewing machine. Now and then Carreras got me a week's work on the subway circuit to pay studio rent and buy costume fabrics. By spring I had five numbers ready.

Carreras announced suddenly, "Inasmuch as you claim to have danced at Teatro Nacional in Mexico City, I am going to make an honest woman of you. The building is still not completed, but I have an engagement for you to dance at the automobile show they are staging there." So Mother and I set out on the long trek south, passing through San Antonio to cross the Rio Grande for my first foreign engagement as an artist.

The first floor of the theater building was given over to the automobile show. A very chic cabaret had been set up on the second floor. I was the featured foreign attraction.

For such occasions Mexican audiences are among the dressiest in the world. Opening night was elegant indeed. Everyone who was anyone in Mexico was there in resplendent evening regalia.

I was scared half to death, yet very proud of my *manola* costume and mantilla of white lace. That pride that we are told goeth before a fall was ready and waiting.

I had never danced on a highly waxed ballroom floor. This and an overtense concentration on making good were to be my undoing.

The orchestra struck up my music; I was introduced; I ran out onto the glassy floor . . . and slipped. Both feet flew into the air. I sat down with a spine-shaking jolt. My tall comb was knocked askew; one castanet shell broke; the heel flew off one shoe . . . What would you have done?

Probably, inasmuch as it was the only thing to do, what I did. I sat there. For about fifteen seconds all of us, audience and I, laughed uproariously. I then picked myself up and limped off.

I went to my dressing room and, while collecting myself generally, changed shoes and castanets.

Again the orchestra went into my music. I ran out as before except that, this time, I felt my toes turning into claws to get a purchase on that terrible floor. I got through the performance with no further mishap. As a first appearance in a very dance-conscious capital it was baroque, but it had one effect not achieved by all first performances—it made us all friends.

From the Auto Club engagement Carreras moved me into the St. Regis Hotel cabaret for several weeks. Mexico City began to supply me with a glamour I had hungered for all my life. My suite was stupefyingly crowded with gigantic baskets of flowers; my days were a whirligig of photographers and interviews. Unexpectedly, Mexico City became the place of my "christening" with the stage name that, having to my mind both logic and charm, has served me agreeably through the intervening decades. It came about so fortuitously as to seem a bit miraculous.

Latins are not notably comfortable with such a Welsh plethora of vowels and silent consonants as my own name, Russell Meriwether Hughes, contained. I myself had felt all along not only that it had a misleading masculine tinge but that it was ill-matched to an artistic career. On first going to New York, I had taken to calling myself Meri Russell Hughes, but that seemed to

have a disagreeable coyness about it. The managers along the
subway circuit hinted rather broadly that it was a too long,
heavy name for an unimportant performer. They cut it down to
Meri Hughes. It remained for an interviewer for one of the Mexico City "slick" weeklies to solve the whole thing. In the first
article she wrote about my performances she simply referred to
me throughout as La Meri. The name appealed to the public,
which quickly took it up. I never cease to be grateful to that
interviewer.

In spite of a crowded schedule of practice, rehearsals and performances, I knew I must also learn. I seized the opportunity to
study Spanish dancing with local teachers.

From a handsome matador, Luis Medina de los Reyes, I took
tauromaquia, the technique of the bullfight. To learn the classic
Mexican dances I went to Pedro Valdez, Mexico's finest native
dancer, who had taught Pavlova and helped her with the staging
of her well-known *Mexican Dances* ballet. Sr. Valdez taught me
the *jarabe tapatío* in its most advanced form.

I was engaged as soloist with the National Symphony Orchestra. I performed several numbers, then Valdez himself partnered
me in my debut in the *jarabe tapatío.* The Mexican audience,
gratified to see a foreign dancer perform the national dance in
classical style, cheered mightily, and the success and resultant
publicity encouraged the newspaper *La Prensa* to engage me to
dance the jarabe in the bullring, with the *orquesta típica,* for a
huge charity show.

Now, of course, every Mexican is, au fond, a jinete, or horse-
man; every *china poblana,* a horsewoman. Naturally, then, my
entrance must be made ariding.

I bustled off to a *hippico* school, where the riding master
selected what appeared to be a fine mount for me. My costume
necessitated riding sidesaddle, which I had never before attempt-
ed. I thought I had better waste no time in learning; my appearance was scheduled for the next day.

I climbed aboard the high-strung little filly. We loped a
couple of times around the ring. With this meager sidesaddled
indoctrination I had to be satisfied.

The next afternoon we galloped out into the bullring, the filly taking the hurdle excitably. The band played loudly; the spectators flung their hats down in a shower all around us.

I am always nervous on a strange horse. Under the calf of my leg I could feel the pounding of the filly's heart. I side-stepped her around the ring under the barrage of hats, and we made our exit over the hurdle.

With what little strength I had left I came back to dance. I sped around the brim of my spanking new sombrero to an exciting ovation, and all went well. When it was over, the riding instructor strolled up and remarked offhand, "You did very well. The filly has never before carried a woman or a sidesaddle . . . or faced a crowd either!" I might have been killed! I opened my mouth to remind him wrathfully of that fact . . . remembering in the nick of time that I must always be a good guest in a foreign country.

We stayed in Mexico three months and were back in New York by late August. I went into a "flash act"—a showy vaudeville specialty—titled *Sevilla,* which Mr. Carreras built around two singers. One of them was launching her career and put up the money for sets and costumes.

As featured dancer I was billed as Queen of the Spanish Shawl, for I had now mastered the handling of the big, heavily embroidered Spanish *manton* in the manner of the bullfighter's cape work, adding a few acrobatic swings of my own invention. My presentation number was a castanet dance in the lace *manola* dress. Then, in opera-length hose and short pants, I came back to manipulate the shawl.

Sevilla was booked on Keith time and in New York opened at the old Hippodrome. The trade press did very nicely by me . . . in a somewhat oblique way. "La Meri is a girl with a perfect understanding," said one, "and she gives us the benefit of it in full-length tights."

Mr. Carreras was pushing me mightily; and since he was inconceivably astute where publicity was concerned, scarcely a paper in New York omitted pictures of me. Alas, he reckoned without the certainty that the prima donna's amour-propre would be ruffled. After several weeks of meeting my face in every paper she picked up she went into a tantrum and closed the act, taking with her the set and costumes. Thus ended *Sevilla.*

Fox Movietone News did a slow-motion film of my *Shawl Dance,* which they showed all over the country. Mother and I were two of their best patrons, spending long hours in the Capitol Theatre, seeing the film over and over again.

Still as Queen of the Spanish Shawl I was booked as a Spanish Star at a rather astounding salary into the Brooklyn Theatre, where, some months previous, I had danced "behind" Maria Montero. I went into a nightclub for a couple of weeks with a group "behind" *me.* I dubbed them the La Meri Girls. We danced Oriental and Spanish numbers, and I walked around the floor, twanging away on a guitar, singing Spanish songs.

During these fill-in engagements my manager had not been idle. By January 1927 he placed me in the Shuberts' *Night in Spain,* a star-studded revue with Ted Healy, Georgie Price, Grace Hayes, Helen Kane, Vanessi, the Gertrude Hoffman Girls, and a host of others. We rehearsed every day, all day, and far into the night. Mr. Shubert could not get along with Mr. Carreras and had it put in my contract that my manager was never to show himself at all, at rehearsals or backstage.

A Night in Spain was fourteen weeks on the road. Although I had originally contracted to dance two Spanish solos, the inevitable reshaping during the break-in weeks brought me more and more chores. A rehearsal was called after the show practically every night, and nearly every rehearsal turned up a new part for me to play. I had no compliant, for every new job was a joyful challenge to me. It never entered my head to ask for more money for more work. I was only too happy that Mr. Shubert judged me capable of the many things he told me to do. I changed costume in the revue thirteen times; I spoke the prologue in Spanish; I sang songs with the chorus line behind me; I played *torero* to Grace Hayes's song; I appeared in comedy skits with Georgie Price. And my *Shawl Dance* was prepared as a special feature, complete with gold costumes and full stage set.

Yet for all the encouragements, the break-in weeks were a rat race, and I was continually harassed by the many changes in the routines. However, the cheerful teasing and kindness, the philosophical balance of the more experienced show-business people saved my life, and I was never to forget the unfailing kindness and courtesy shown my mother by all the people connected with the show, including Mr. Shubert.

I had felt nervous, wondering if she should be with me. Stage mothers have been known to be expendable. But Mother had her own code. She made it a rule never to attend a rehearsal. Though traveling with me, she never once went backstage; instead she always waited patiently at the stage door to accompany me home. She never heckled me with advice or criticism. One thing she dearly wanted was for me to learn to stand on my own feet in the world. She stood to one side deliberately, cheering me on with an occasional quiet compliment if the going got too tough. In other words, she was the exact antithesis of the fluttering, meddlesome, battling stage mother. She didn't take for granted the treatment accorded her. She earned it.

Two weeks before the show was to open in New York we were playing Philadelphia early in a cold, rainy March. On a Friday night Mother was waiting as usual at the stage door to take me home. She got damp-through from walking in the sleeted streets. The stage door hallway was cold and draughty. Saturday morning she awoke feeling very ill. I called the house doctor, then, at her insistence, went on to the matinee. By nightfall her temperature was so high that she was delirious, calling with pitiful insistence for her own mother. By Sunday the fever had subsided, and both she and the doctor thought it better to go to New York, where her own physician could take care of her.

I didn't want to leave her Monday to rejoin the company, but she seemed better, and Dr. Freed felt that my missing work would trouble her more than my presence would help. So, leaving her in the capable and loving hands of the doctor and a nurse, I caugnt up with the company in New England. Every evening about five I would call her long distance for a chat. For a few days she seemed much better. But one evening when I was talking with her, her mind began to wander. A few hours later Dr. Freed advised me to go to New York immediately. The company was wonderful to me, getting me a reservation, helping me to pack, seeing me off.

The pneumonia attack had reached its height and she recognized me only vaguely. The little dog she loved cowered under the bed, refusing to come out to eat or be walked. Through a nightmare of hours doctors and nurses fought for her life, but with the dawn of a mid-March day in 1927 she quietly relinquished her will to live and left us to rejoin her beloved Russ.

The Caribbean

Great plans were afoot. My manager was forming a small company to tour the Caribbean during the summer months. It consisted of an instrumental trio, artists of both experience and reputation; two singers, a baritone and a soprano with, perhaps, less reputation but certainly with experience; and the dancers, a ballet adagio team, two other "girls," and myself. My sister had persuaded her husband to let her come and stay with me for a while after Mother's death, and it proved easy to induce her to be one of the "girls." For the second one we engaged Billy, a very young and pretty member of the chorus that had worked behind me in one of the Brooklyn movie-house engagements. That had been quite a week, and she and I often laughed about it. Having been engaged to perform my *Shawl Dance,* I had swung the shawl about with the carelessness of an inebriated signalman. The jazz orchestra was strung along the rear of the stage, and at one performance the fringe of my shawl had plucked a saxophone from its stand, heaving it out into a startled audience.

Our one month of preparation was pretty hectic. Since my own repertoire amounted only to some six numbers, I had to build more dances both for myself and for the girls, and we had to make costumes, for they would be impossibly expensive to have made.

At last we embarked for Havana. The trip down was beautiful—at least I think it was, for I was in a dream beyond dreaming. First dancer in a company en route to foreign climes! I was blissfully unaware of frictions and undercurrents already beginning to flow among other members of the company.

We opened at the Payret Theater in Havana. Between performances and endless hours of rehearsal I saw little of the beautiful city.

35

When our engagement at the Payret closed, we went inland to a couple of smaller towns. The more sophisticated of our company found the primitive hotels rather more than quaint. Ventilation, for example, was created by not carrying the walls to ceiling height. No thought was given to audio privacy. Our Russian adagio dancer discovered a large and demonstrative tarantula on her wall, and her screams were such as to shame a locomotive. My sister and I were less beset. Our Texas training proved invaluable. We ordered a broom. When the creatures appeared on the walls, we brushed them off, stepped on them, and went to sleep.

I was not always so successful in dealing with the human fauna. The overly zealous *piropos*—compliments, to put it more kindly—of the Cuban equivalent of drugstore cowboy annoyed me. One day when several of them followed me, I became alarmed. My studiedly dignified walk accelerated until it became a nervous trot. With relief I reached the hotel. My tormentors followed me in. I complained to the desk clerk. To him, discretion was evidently very much the better part of valor. As this comet's tail of undesirables now numbered at least a score and was growing, the clerk declined to order them from the lobby. In a near panic I started up the broad staircase. Two of the crowd bounded after me.

At that moment, like the legendary U.S. Marines, Mr. Carreras materialized at the top of the stairs. Some well-chosen, if not very refined, remarks were showered down on the men by my knight. Other members of our company, housed on the second floor, caught the rising racket of shouts and rushed out to reinforce our side. A little emboldened now, the reluctant desk clerk got around to calling police. Waiting for them to arrive, Carreras, the Russian cellist, and the Italian pianist held back the mob, impaling it on red-hot points of diatribe.

In a town that size the scandal was on everybody's tongue by nightfall, time for our opening concert. A police escort to the theater was forced on us. In spite of it—or perhaps because of it—I was frightened half to death as we drove through the pitch-dark streets.

We had an audience, but it was not large and certainly not unbearably enthusiastic. However, protected by the gimlet-eyed watchfulness of the police, we made it to the final curtain with no extreme *crise de nerfs* or in fact any reaction from the audience worse than indifference. When our train pulled out of Santa Clara en route to Santiago de Cuba, I, for one, was in a fine mood.

In Ponce we had our little encounter with a Peeping Tom. Lovely little Ponce with its Gay Nineties firehouse, its jasmine-covered cathedral, its singing lizards, its rides in the surrey with the fringe on top for the magnificent sum of 25 cents an hour!

In Cuba in those days peepholes in the dressing rooms were de rigueur. The first job of any visiting artist was to stop up the holes with wads of cleansing tissue or hanging clothes; or if the holes were near the floor, with suitcases. Shoes were no good, for they had a way of walking, apparently under their own power.

My dressing room in Ponce looked out onto a patio and was shuttered. I stopped all discernible holes. Still, as I put on my makeup, I had a queasy sense of bold eyes taking a good look-see.

Indignantly I located Carreras and demanded immediate measures. He strode out into the patio, taking care to make no noise, and sure enough, a dark, crouching figure had eyes glued to the shutters of my dressing room. Silently Carreras fetched a fearful kick to the seat of the pants.

And who did our Peeping Tom turn out to be? None other than the regular critic of the town's leading newspaper! I am sure there is a moral somewhere in the incident, but I have never quite decided what it is.

I had been assured that there were not only pirates in the Caribbean but mermaids too, so I was on the lookout for them. I found my pirates before leaving Cuba. At least they looked like pirates. They wore red scarves around their heads and red and white striped knee-length pants. I didn't count their number, but their aggregate strength appalled me. Bending their broad brown backs and muscled arms to stowing bags of sugar

in the hold of our ship, in twenty-four consecutive hours they
loaded sixty thousand pounds.

A different breed of pirate, a gang I never actually saw or
heard identified, gave me a more personal sample of their calling.
When we unpacked for customs in Puerto Rico, we found, where
our four Spanish shawls should have been, newspapers! Quick
search revealed that a good haul had been made in what, I am
sure, the misguided "pirates" believed were valuable articles,
among them a prop "diamond" ring, a huge and flashy affair—
price $6.

After a very rough voyage on a very bad ship the landlocked
harbor of San Juan de Puerto Rico looked like paradise. "Good
old terra firma," we muttered, ashen-lipped. Only the other day
I noticed a full-page color ad about "romantic, old-world San
Juan." The text mentioned massive hotels with modern appointments, overlooking the city, modern department stores, and all
manner of sophisticated fixings.

The San Juan at which we arrived on that tour was a hodge-
podge of mongrel architecture, of narrow cobbled streets debouching into unexpected and deserted plazas. Noise was continuous, high-pitched, and deafening. Jalopy drivers never ceased
tooting their horns, finding it less effort than using brakes and
more fun as well. Even church bells rang with a tempo that
made the effect hysterical.

San Juan was not notably interested in theater. Our houses
were only fair, though one critic unbent enough to say, "This
Teatro de las Artes seems to us very good. But then, how can
we tell? We have never had anything down here to compare it
with."

However, San Juan was interested in poetry, women, wine,
and horses, in that order. In San Juan every man is a poet,
from the lawyer in his chambers to the policeman at the crossing. Any business conference or financial deal will be suspended
at any time in the greater interest of reciting poetry. For the
sake of box office, therefore, mounting my carousel mustang of
verse once more, I had the satisfaction of seeing verse of mine in
print in the San Juan daily press, translated by no less a poet

than Mr. Lorens-Torres! In the end, however, the troupe and I
came to realize that, in San Juan, the Atteneo and the Public
Library drew better houses than the Municipal Theatre and even
the Casino.

Our company fell on evil days. What with money running
low and the calendar drawing toward fall, the musicians and
singers announced they were leaving us, sailing for New York.

The dancing contingent worked on until one day our Russian
adagio lady was asked by Carreras to wait for her salary. Bitter
words flew back and forth. However well known it is that there
is no blood in the onion, the lady stopped her ears to such logic,
flouncing away in a great huff. Just as we were sitting down to
lunch she flounced back, leading the chief of police, and had
Carreras arrested. I must say that as we watched our last remaining male bulwark being led away to jail, Lilian, Billy, and I
were thoroughly scared.

We were further confused when, before we could decide to at
least drink our coffee, our manager sauntered back and sat down
again at the table with his guest, the chief of police. The two
gentlemen then proceeded with lunch, enthusiastically discussing
the fine points of Dante.

An hour later, smiling around at all of us graciously, the
police chief took his leave. All was once more as it had been
before our Russian colleague had given vent to her impetuous
outburst. That is, it was until departure time for the next U.S.-
bound boat. Aboard was our coldly indignant adagio couple.
Of our original *Teatro de las Artes* company of twelve, there remained in San Juan now only three dancers and an impresario
out of money.

We pulled in our belts. Lilian was delegated to hold all cash
and ordered not to let a cent above our painfully meager budget
out of her grasp until we had somehow made and saved enough
to leave. Our lunches consisted of two-for-a-nickel avocados, our
suppers of spaghetti cooked on the gas burner in the room Lilian,
Billy, and I shared. We swore off all forms of entertainment involving so much as trolley fare.

Meanwhile Carreras hustled around and got the three of us a

dancing job in the local movie house. I say "dancing." Of our *Teatro de las Artes* repertoire, little but the Spanish numbers had enough popular appeal to hold our job. Quickly Lilian and I revived some of the songs and ukulele numbers we had done for the troops during the war; Billy put together a tap routine.

At the rate we were going, I must say it bade fair to be at least ten years before we saved enough money to buy passages for four. But fate had another little surprise for us. Billy got tropical fever.

We had no money for doctors or the hospital. Lilian jumped to the rescue. She called the U.S. Army Hospital and by mentioning her Army husband with broad old-school-tie implications she sweet-talked the commanding major into taking Billy in. Happily, the unidentified fever ran its course in two or three days.

Billy was no sooner restored to her shaky pins than I got a like fever. Again the major gave a wink of the official eye and I was trundled on a stretcher into the tall, cool hospital. My fever proved stubborn. Day dragged after day. I was so afraid that I wouldn't be able to dance as soon as I got out that when the nurses' backs were turned, I sneaked into the bathroom and practiced, to keep in shape.

Returning from one of these sneak practice sessions, I fell on my face in a faint, bloodying my nose and loosening a couple of teeth. The justly irate nurse did what she could to convince me how stupid I was.

It seemed months that I floated through days and nights at that hospital. I was getting no better. No one had been able to identify the fever. Then one day the major arrived hurriedly, his kindly face grave and anxious. He went into whispered confab with the nurse, who began immediately to fill me with enough big quinine pills to cure a lion. That evening, weak as a wet rag but free of fever, I departed the hospital. The pressing need for my immediate cure was simple. The poor major had been notified that the commandant colonel was arriving on an inspection of the hospital. Was the major to be found harboring a civilian who had no right whatsoever to be within a governmental installation?

It was pretty obvious that I could not work for some time, so the sooner we got out of that climate, the better off we'd be. We put together what we'd saved by scrimping and it was enough to buy three passages on the cheapest freighter bound for the States. Three passages and four people? It was finally decided mutually that Carreras would wait in Puerto Rico until Lilian and I could get home and borrow passage money to wire to him.

So we bade farewell to our financially landlocked manager and boarded the old S.S. *Lake Fairport,* which carried us back to the States on what was to be her last trip. She boasted no wireless; her few lifeboats looked anything but seaworthy. The young captain must have been bedeviled by some personal tragedy, for he was seldom, if ever, sober. The sailors were a raffish lot, and Lilian, Billy, and I were the only passengers. The stage seemed set for some episode of outlandishness. None developed. It was a good object lesson in the truth that people and circumstances often prove better than they look.

The rusty, wallowing old freighter took her time leaving the islands for her state-side port, Mobile. She stopped at every port around the entire island of Puerto Rico. She paused in the beautiful landlocked harbor of Santo Domingo. But at last we left the islands, pointing for home. Haiti's rugged coast rolled away like drifting clouds of heavy autumn smoke. Soon we were in open sea, a hostile sea, rough and rain-tossed. But there were still the flying fishes, the jokester porpoises, and once the full, double arch of a brilliant tropic rainbow sprang suddenly from the horizon to one side of the boat, burying itself in the horizon on the other side.

Through the uneasy Gulf we sailed and up the Mississippi finally into the port of Mobile. The customs officials welcomed a little break in monotony. Never having been called upon to handle anything like our trunkfuls of costumes, they were delighted, even donning our hula skirts to give an impromptu dance, which we applauded, not without an eye to the practical. We had been afraid there would be trouble, red tape, duty we could not pay—and we got hula dancers! It was not our first or last time of discovering that nothing is so unpredictable as a customs official.

Mobile had a wonderful slice of good fortune for us. Don Philippini was conducting the orchestra at one of the big movie houses. His wife, who had given me my first professional job in San Antonio, listened with the sympathetic ear of the born trouper to our tale of woe. The theater was booked for weeks ahead, but she briskly engaged Lilian and Billy for a two-week stint in the near future and advanced them their pay. God bless her!

With these "pennies from heaven" we hurried on to San Antonio in style, otherwise known as Pullman accommodations. We had to have a place where we could stay, and we had to get Carreras out of bondage. We borrowed money from a longtime banker friend and wired it to our manager with news of our whereabouts. Then Lilian and I plunged into the business of opening our big house. Our spirits revived. Giving the house a lick-and-a-promise cleaning, we plunged into a round of rollicking homecoming parties.

In two weeks Carreras arrived at our door. Within five minutes he announced that our partying was now over and we would give a concert immediately in San Antonio. What else? Were we to walk to New York?

Obediently we three went into rehearsal. Our manager rented Beethoven Hall for a date in early December and swung into high gear on his publicity campaign. As for Lilian and me, somehow it seemed natural and very pleasant to be working again in our old dance hall in the basement.

Our performance went well. The leading San Antonio critic gave me a restrained word of praise for my "exceptional costumes"—a phrase destined to be used by other critics hundreds of times later in my career.

On the strength of the concert the local movie palace engaged us for two weeks. We had sufficient resources now to get us all back to New York by train. Lilian and Billy stopped off in Mobile to fulfill their obligation to Mrs. Philippini.

The year 1928 was still young when we moved into a little

theatrical hotel just off Broadway. My destiny was not settled. I was on my way to becoming a concert dancer. We plunged into the training, not the least of which were more movie-house and nightclub engagements, to make the wherewithal for living.

Lilian's Dave, stationed again in the States, came to retrieve his wife. Undoubtedly she felt some trepidation at leaving me unchaperoned. For herself, however, a rest and change from all the unknown quantities would not be unwelcome.

South America—1928

I made my debut as a solo concert dancer at the John Golden Theatre in New York on a Sunday, May 6, 1928. Exactly one month previous Carreras had simply told me, without elaboration, that he had engaged the theater and it was therefore up to me to prepare the program. Not only was I undaunted, I was happily enthused. Any new project always seized all my attention and energy, and this project was one that activated a dream. I plunged into creation and re-creation of the various dances, and I wrote Lilian to come with all undeliberate speed and help me with making the costumes.

The very air of New York at that time was a stimulus to creative work. I do not believe any other decade has produced so many creative, sometimes iconoclastic, dance artists. Many were Denishawn-trained, but World War I had engendered a rebellion against romanticism, also against the courtly exactitude of ballet. In Germany Mary Wigman led the way, and with the artistic truths of shadowy Isadora Duncan spurring them on, several gallant pioneers fought for the right of the individual artist to express himself as he elected. Doris Humphrey and Charles Weidman, Martha Graham, Agnes De Mille, and a host of others were drawing about them dedicated students and giving as many performances as finances allowed to whatever public might appear. Broadway theaters being available on Sundays, each week several of these consecrated and courageous artists appeared. In the beginning of this renaissance the dancers were reviewed by music and drama critics. Gradually, by their very numbers and strength, they brought about the engagement of regular dance critics on the staffs of the city's papers.

Having started my personal career a bit lower down on the caste scale, namely "show biz," I knew none of these vestals personally, was not even on the fringe of their aesthetic world. Yet I drew courage from their courage, creating most of my dances myself in a free lyric style that was natural to me. Not forgetting my earlier devotion to Euterpe, I presented two numbers to an accompaniment of poetry reading—William Rose Benet's "Pale Dancer" and "Morgiana Dances." Only a few dances of ethnic content were choreographed by others than myself. I was accompanied by the young pianist Fred Bristol, himself something of an iconoclast.

I cannot claim to have drawn a very large audience, but friends, flowers, and applause made it seem very glamorous and myself an "arrived artist." The critics were divided but not unkind, and Charles Isaacson gave me a column of unqualified approval. His judgment was a benison of encouragement as I went about preparing for a South American tour that was to begin on June 1.

On such a tour, made up as it is of seasons in a town, against one-night stands, it is necessary to take a minimum of three complete programs. And so in the few weeks I had for preparation I worked with Michio Ito on repertoire, besides creating new dances myself, in the meantime frantically cutting and sewing costumes with the help of a neighbor and my sister.

Money that Mother had willed to me in the form of life insurance to establish my concert career went into a black velvet cyclorama, a gray floorcloth, numerous spotlights, the lessons, and costume materials. The last of it went into steamship passages for this, my first solo tour. I was humbly conscious of the moral debt I owed my mother's memory. In losing her I had paid an enormous price, however indirectly, for this career of mine, and I was determined to make of my life a success of which she could be proud.

And so our little company of four—Carreras, Bristol, Lilian, whose husband again "loaned" her to me, and I—set out from New York to essay the world.

We arrived in La Guaira, Venezuela, on a June morning just

when the sun was touching the incredible mountains with misty pastel shades. Anchored far out in the harbor, the ship was so motionless that it seemed to be sharing my own breathless excitement. Presently a shining launch, filled with official-looking men, cut a spumed path from pier to ship. Gold-laced officers came aboard smartly—and asked for me! This was the reception committee with which President Vincent Gomez welcomed any artist bringing culture to his country. So it was not without some pomp that I disembarked, surrounded by military "brass" and laden with flowers. All customs formalities were dispensed with, and we hurtled up the winding, dangerous road to the capital in a cavalcade of black Cadillacs.

Caracas of some fifty years ago was a city drowsy and sun-drenched. The streets were narrow and cobbled, the buildings painted in pastels of pink and green. Squat, Spanish in style, they turned blank facades, marked by barred windows, to the street, for the life of the occupants centered on sunny patios within.

Only the most discreet of signs identified our hotel from neighboring homes. Its big patio was lush with tropic growth, and along the second floor, which housed the guests, a gallery overlooked the rioting colors of the garden.

Our performances were in the National Theatre, a huge frame building that has received many of the great artists of the past twenty years: Duncan, Pavlova, Schumann-Heink, Paderewski, and a host of others. The President did not stop with a bouquet for my first performance; he sent one for each. For each dinner in the hotel came a magnum of champagne from the same donor.

At the close of our two-month season in Caracas President Gomez invited me for a special performance in his summer palace in Maracay, and it was there that I finally met this extraordinary man. He invited me to his gardens for tea so that I might admire his collection of rare white peacocks.

Himself an Indian, he was very shy of social formalities. Yet as he showed us around he seemed easy and happy. Quite untutored in arts and cultures, he would sit in absorbed

contemplation of the beauty of the white fowl as they paraded
the jade-green lawns, spreading their ghostly tails.

Of the single performance there at the summer palace I have
rather mixed memories. The floor of the stage was of an un-
evenness rivaling the brooding Andes. The piano was so out of
tune that I was never quite sure what dance Fred Bristol was
playing. But the private audience was generous, the President
enthusiastically pleased, and the resulting check, together with
the gift of a wristwatch, enormous!

Whereas Caracas and Maracay were bucolic and simple, in the
twenties Maracaibo was a mess! Arriving by boat late at night,
we sloshed through unpaved, unlighted streets thick with tropic
mud. The best hotel in town proved to be only a slight step
above a flophouse. Our entire party (we had added a young
Venezuelan lad, Landaeta, as stage assistant) was assigned to one
big room. Indeed, we discovered that it was only in deference
to our artistic station that we were not asked to share our quarters with several strangers.

We huddled in a corner of the dreadful room while Carreras
rushed out to try to arrange something more plausible. By
going as far as the governor of the province, he finally found
rooms for Lilian and me in a private home.

My performance the next night was, to say the least, unusual.
I danced in the State Theatre. Since it was opened only for
companies of high artistic value, it had stood closed for a long
time. I asked myself, who, other than ourselves, would go to
Maracaibo?

I shared my solo program with a democratic collection of bats
and rats, which scurried happily about the stage, ignoring the
performance but causing consternation among the lily-livered
foreign artists. There was an interesting extra added attraction.
It was some saint's day and the governor, sitting attentively in
the stage box, had to call out soldiers to stop the audience from
shooting off firecrackers in the aisle. All in all, I think I gave
the most courageous and least artistic performance of my life.

In those far days one did not take a Boeing 707 to go from
Maracaibo to Barranquilla. Indeed, one did not even take a

coastwise steamer—because there was none. The way to make
the trip was to go to Curaçao and loaf around until a boat
sauntered through bound for Colombia.

However, nobody minds going to Curaçao. It is small and
windswept, as neat as Holland, as colorful as Trinidad. We spent
our free days swimming in warm, blue seas and browsing through
breezy shops.

We gave one performance in Curaçao while we were awaiting a
boat. It took place on the small dais of a private country club.
The Dutch audience, small in numbers but massive in tonnage,
enjoyed the show from the luxury of wicker armchairs. The
performance was nearly over before we grasped that an eerie
moaning we had heard all evening was the plaintive protesting of
those wicker chairs.

In Barranquilla we were booked for a Sunday matinee at the
Colombo Theatre. There was a large American colony in the
city, connected with the fast-growing oil industry. Sunday
morning, in an excess of southern hospitality, a group of Amer-
icans invited us to a mint-julep party. Happily I do not care for
mint juleps. So much could not be said of either Fred Bristol or
my sister. The matinee was colorful. Bristol played the entire
show without once hitting a right note. How Lilian stayed on
her feet is anybody's guess.

We arrived for our season in Cartagena toward the end of
July. What a beautiful city it was! The streets were sunny and
somnolent, seemingly deserted by all save the ghosts of long-
dead buccaneers. The great stone sea walls, weatherbeaten and
scarred by ancient battles, were unimpaired in strength; green
things grew in their cracks like ever-fresh flower offerings on
gravestones of the past.

The white marble theater, adorned with fading statues in
niches, seemed as asleep as everything else. It impressed itself
on me one sunny afternoon when I climbed, in the company of
a young poet, to the shards of the old fort. Here one felt suspended in a world between earth and heaven, between life and
death. The heads of the flowers bent gently to the salt winds;
the sea was too far away for the sound of creaming waves to be

heard. To the west lifted the inaccessible mountains. At the foot of the hill the city seemed emptied of all life but dreams.

In Panama we gave eleven concerts in August's enervating heat. But all along the Canal Zone we made friends.

Lilian was leaving us here. Her pregnancy was far advanced. Dave had gotten leave to come down and take her back to the States.

I left Panama the poorer by the absence of my sister, the richer by having learned the native dance, the tamborito, for which I had acquired a typical costume, the pollera.

We set off for Costa Rica in a small, rickety freighter. I was tired enough to go straight to my bunk and sleep soundly through the storm that raged all night and threatened seriously to send us to the bottom.

At the tiny port of San José de Costa Rica we were met by a private train that took us up into the capital. The little engine, pulling a baggage car with our luggage and one coach with our company of four, chugged sturdily through the endless banana trees to deposit us at last at our destination. The whole city was as delightful as a little operetta, and loveliest of all was the theater. Built of marble, it was a small reproduction of the Teatro Colón in Buenos Aires. It was fully equipped for large opera companies, few of which had been there.

Nothing is ever perfect, but the imperfections of the National Theatre, while not unusual in a tropic climate, were far from pleasant. Backstage was alive with bedbugs! We used hogsheads of Flit before, during, and after every performance. And the night we packed up to leave we turned all our spotlights onto center stage; I "flitted" and packed costumes alternately while the men of the company stood by watchfully, ready with weapons to slaughter any of the enemy that tried to flee.

Hoping we were not carrying any stowaways, wearily we boarded our train and set out through a stormy night for the port. The weather was awful; our boat was delayed. We huddled to wait in the comfortless wet dark. All the "take" of our highly successful season in San José was in my manager's briefcase.

At long last the little steamer came gasping up to take us aboard from the rickety pier. Carreras hurried to the wireless room to request the Italian steamer with which we were to connect in Panama to wait for us—three first-class passengers, one second-class, and six tons of luggage. (I do not exaggerate in saying six tons.)

When morning dawned, we were still far from our destination. And what should Carreras discover but that his briefcase was missing! In other words, our funds were not aboard! All told we might have had as much as twenty dollars in pocket money among us, and we were due for an engagement in Lima! No doubt the briefcase had been stolen in the darkness on the pier.

"Never mind," said Carreras, "we will make it." I forbore to ask how.

Our tired little tramp boat struggled up to the pier in Panama where the big S.S. *Orazio,* steam up, was most impatiently awaiting us. Amid highly articulate excitement we rushed aboard, standing at the rail to watch cranes snatch our luggage up in nets and dump it into the hold. The first-class passengers stood by, staring at us with curiosity. At least we were important enough to keep a liner waiting for us three long hours.

Before the deckhands had the hatches covered, we put out to sea. Only then did Carreras go to the captain and tell him frankly that we had no money. So the La Meri Company traveled from Panama to Callao, Peru, steerage.

Happily the ship was not crowded and I had a six-berth cabin to myself. Happily too it was a fine new boat, spic and span, with separate tables in the dining salon. Since no one on earth eats better than the Italian peasant, our food was delicious. Frankly, it was great fun. Our fellow passengers were cheery and full of song. To dress for dinner they changed from a white undershirt to a red one. The sea was calm, the days were sunny, and the steerage deck of a good liner is a good deal more comfortable than the freighter decks I have known from time to time. Furthermore, when movies were shown in the first-class lounge, the deck steward would sneak us in to watch them. Overall, it was a delightful adventure. When we finally anchored

in Callao, we sailed jauntily up to the first-class deck to receive
the reporters and photographers who came aboard for us. I am
sure many a first-class passenger wondered where we had kept
ourselves during the voyage.

How I love Lima! We had been there two weeks; my ten
concerts had been received with gratifying success. I shall not
forget the thrilling compliment paid me the day after I first presented my *La Corrida* dance. I was sitting at luncheon in the
hotel dining room when a dark, ugly, but infinitely graceful man
came to our table. With stately formality he offered felicitations
on my performance, adding, "It is *thus* that the bullfight should
be danced!" How I treasured his words when I found that he
was a famous *torero* recently arrived from Spain.

By now it was mid-October and Fred Bristol had to return to
the States to fulfill contracts as concert accompanist to Lucrezia
Bori. So I gave no more concerts in Lima. Yet I could not
bring myself to leave. Besides, I had been invited to dance in
the annual presentation of *The Vision of Viracotcho.* This was a
reconstruction of the ancient Inca festivals as they were before
the arrival of the Spaniards. It was quite unprecedented for a
foreigner to appear in the production, so imagine my delight, in
accepting, to learn that I was to dance the two solos of the
Flecha and the *Onda.*

A professor of Incan culture, himself an Inca, taught me the
dances and helped me assemble examples of the ancient
garments.

The performance was in the National Theatre and was accompanied by the symphony orchestra. A keen sense of responsibility made me tense, so much so that I moved as in a dream and
afterward could remember little of the details of the evening
save that when, during the *Flecha,* I, as an Indian from Guayaquil, found myself surrounded by stern Incan spearmen, I was
truly frightened.

All my days on tour fell into a pattern of self-inflicted
schedule. All morning I rehearsed in the theater. All afternoon
I kept to my room. In the evenings I performed, or on nonper-
formance days, dined and went straight back to my room. I

whiled away my solitary afternoons and evenings by writing a
long narrative poem on the fall of the Incan Empire. In some
way this poem was brought to the attention of the incumbent
president of Peru. I was asked to call at the Presidential Palace.

The interview was delightfully informal. The President said it
was his intention to publish my poem under government auspices.
He made plans for elaborate decoration of the book with plates
of existing artwork of the Incas.

Alas, within a few months after our departure the regime was
overthrown and my literary protector flung into prison. To this
day my poem remains unpublished.

In late October we set sail for Chile. As a replacement for
Fred Bristol we took along Mo. Cendalli, an Argentinian pianist,
also a conductor who had orchestrated all my numbers. En
route to Santiago we stopped and gave four concerts in two
coast towns, Iquique and Antofagosta. Both were mining towns
built on the narrow, barren strip between the Pacific and the
lowering Andes. In that wasteland it seemed little short of a
miracle to receive a great sheaf of red and yellow carnations as
homage to my Spanish dances.

Something very near a miracle, too, was Cendalli's handling of
the orchestra. In one town the first violinist, by day a barber,
was self-taught; moreover, he had taught himself left-handed!
And we were using compositions of Ravel, Griffes, Debussy,
Schumann, Albéniz, et al.!

Although extremely happy, I was close to exhaustion a good
part of the time. Performances ran for an hour and three quarters with only one intermission. I had made myself so expert at
changing that I was never offstage more than three minutes between numbers. And the whole show was just me. I had sewn
my costumes with a careful eye to quick changes, and they, with
the shoes and jewelry to go with them, were laid out carefully
across my many trunks, for there was no time to be lost in
taking them down from hangers. An evening's performance was,
therefore, grueling work; but I was sustained by my love of the
theater, my dreams of the future, and that out-of-time-and-space
catalysis every artist feels when the curtain goes up. And then,

at the end of every exhausting season, there would be a lazy
boat trip to recharge my system.

Santiago de Chile was certainly the pinnacle in glamour of
that first Latin American tour. Booked for three concerts at the
National Theatre, I gave thirteen. In the great rehearsal hall of
the building I spent the mornings making new repertoire, in
many ways always the happiest time of a dancer's life.

So popular did I become that paper sellers and fruit venders
refused to accept payment from the members of my company.
I appeared on newsreels, broadcast on radio, rode on a drag hunt
that the Club Hippico gave in my honor, swam and dived in the
aquatic meet, and received banks of flowers and miles of press.
The great Perez-Freire even wrote a *cueca* for me. In short,
everything went much the way Hollywood pictures stage
"success."

During my season in Santiago a series of earthquakes shook
the southern part of Chile. Nearly every night we would feel
the violent tremors in the capital. The Chilenos took them
calmly enough and when the chandeliers began to shake they
would merely pick up their coffee cups and go out into the street
without interrupting their conversations. I am not of such sturdy
stuff. The first night I felt the tremors and saw my bedroom
door straining its lintel, I leaped up and ran down five flights of
stairs and into the street without benefit of robe to cover my
pajamas of rousing pink. On performance nights I insisted that
the big sliding doors behind the backdrop be kept open for my
immediate flight. Gradually, however, I grew acclimated and began to sleep quietly through those shakeups. During the worst
of the earth's seizures the entire southern town of Talca was
destroyed. We put on two shows in full benefit for the earthquake sufferers. I was already a "darling of the public," but this
upped my popularity another notch. President-elect Herbert
Hoover, on a goodwill tour of South America, arrived in Chile
during those days. Imagine my delight when he wrote me, in
longhand, commending my help in inter-American friendship. A
few days later I met Mr. Hoover and his beautiful wife at a gala
reception given by the American ambassador.

We spent Christmas at Peñaflor, a summer resort near Santiago. It was a midsummer Christmas to us, with the festive tree standing among the tall eucalyptus trees. The vacation was not long, but it was very welcome; I forgot all about dancing for a while and swam in the river and rode horseback.

My career, I felt, was going brilliantly. I had met every challenge and, by dint of endless hours of joyous work, had overcome them.

Toward mid-January of 1929 we crossed the snow-crested Andes and the sun-drenched pampas and I caught my first glimpse of Buenos Aires, that "Paris of America." There Carreras made arrangements for March engagements and we went on to Brazil, where we played several seasons in several towns, finding the public both cultured and hospitable. In beautiful Sâo Paulo we met with an unusual custom. It was necessary to give a full-dress rehearsal for the police department before we opened. Even the Pavlova company had met this requirement. Upon inquiry I found that the ruling had been made after a performance by Tortola Valencia, who achieved fame in Reinhardt's *Sumurun*. Tortola was a *gitana pura*; she had been known to horsewhip a critic publicly in retaliation for an unfavorable review. She had a fabulous collection of Spanish shawls, and it was her custom to don a different shawl for each bow demanded by her public. One night the Sâo Paulo "gallery gods" decided to find out just how many shawls she had and kept her bowing for a long time before she guessed that they were pulling her leg. She came to the end of her shawls at last and reappeared in the one she had worn to take the first bow. Shouting that they had already seen that shawl, the gallery gods continued to clap, whereupon Tortola lost her temper and strode out on the stage au naturel. In the ensuing uproar no one heard what she said, but all saw the gestures she made! An insulted public began throwing whatever objects were handy; the management nervously rang down the metal fire curtain; and Tortola, clad only in a shawl, made a hasty escape by carriage.

We gave a season at the end of February in the *muy simpatico* city of Montevideo, then crossed the river to Buenos Aires. Our

hotel was on the Calle Esmeralda. It was the custom to close
this street at five in the afternoon to all but pedestrian traffic.
Here the beaux of the town congregated to watch the belles pass
and to give them the *piropo*, the Spanish audible compliment—
sometimes in verse—to the charms of the lady. We were to learn
soon that in Buenos Aires the *piropo* sometimes descended to
pinching. One lady, a tourist, thus *piropoed*, struck her compli-
menter with her handbag. The outraged beau had her arrested
for assault and battery. Furthermore, the judge fined her!
Some years later a law was passed prohibiting "pinching where it
hurts." But in 1929 I was mortally afraid of *piropos*, even the
relatively innocent spoken kind, and, like many a Latin miss,
hated to walk in the streets alone. Time changes us all. When I
returned to Buenos Aires ten years later, I confess I garnered
each word tossed to me, treasuring it eagerly.

My concerts were given in a charming *intime* theater, the
Odeon. On alternate nights the stage was taken by the great
actor Alexander Moissi and his company. It was a great honor
and pleasure to meet this charming artist and his gifted wife.
He admired my work and suggested that he propose to Reinhardt to engage me for some European appearances. With such
a prospect looming before me like a benignant augury, I attacked
the last four months of my South American tour with vigor and
joy.

On little river boats we chugged up the glossy waters of the
Rio Paraná; Lomas de Zamora, Córdoba, Rio Quatro, Villa
María, Santa Fe, Paraná, Corrientes, Resistencia, Saénz Peña,
Posadas, Concordia, Salto, Gualeguaychú, Asunción—I danced in
them all. I cannot remember in which of these fair cities I was
required to call at the editorial offices of a certain newspaper for
an interview. Social form is rather strict in Argentina, and a
visiting artist must be extremely careful of her behavior, lest it
be misunderstood. I declined the honor and suggested that the
interviewer come to my hotel. The editor, feeling much put
out, was scathing in his review of my debut, expressing the
opinion that my hula was "vulgar." To our surprise the local
Catholic paper took up the cudgels in my favor and declared the

hula as I danced it a model of naive charm. With each issue of
each paper the war of words built up. Of course, all this fortuitous publicity reflected at the box office. We stayed quite a
long while in that town.

We visited another town that was a real outpost of civilization.
It was an oil-boom town, with unpaved streets deep in mire,
lined with shacks constructed of tin and unpainted lumber. The
hotel had mud floors, and the legs of the beds were set in pans
of kerosene to keep the insect life at a respectful distance. Kerosene lamps stood in for electric lights; one unsavory outhouse
did yeoman service in lieu of plumbing. The odoriferous town
dump, filled with carcasses of overworked horses and mules, was
two short blocks from the main street. The only decent building
in town was the new theater.

As was to be expected, most of the town's inhabitants were
rough workmen. On the night of my one performance the classic section of my program drew only polite applause from the
full house. But when I appeared in Spanish costume, I was
greeted with cacophonous sound—whistles, shouts, and remarks
not too refined in nature. I left the stage insulted and in tears.
Carreras left his spotlights and went out and told the public to
behave itself. Words hurtled back and forth, not to mention
threats and curses. The mayor hurried backstage and demanded
that Carreras apologize to the public. This he refused to do, so
they took him off to spend the night in jail.

A group of schoolteachers came back and begged me to complete the performance. As most of the rowdies had queued up
to enjoy Carreras's progress to the jail, I complied, not without
trepidation. With the greatest pleasure we caught an early boat
the next morning.

Without doubt the highlight of our river trip was Asunción.
Not in years had an artist visited this capital city of Paraguay.
Besides being isolated, the country had been at war for so long
that money was very scarce and most of the people could hardly
afford to buy shoes for their feet. My arrival was a sensation.

We announced one concert, but during the intermission every
seat was sold out for a second. After five performances we

found ourselves so affluent that we decided to take time out for a hunting trip up in the Chaco.

We rented a small motor launch and, early one June morning, set out up the river. The party consisted of Carreras, myself, Cendalli, three members of our local orchestra, and three hunting dogs. It was the dark hour before dawn when we started across the wide water that laves Asunción. Halfway across, the dogs began to whine and move about, and we discovered that our little boat, greatly overloaded, was shipping water to an alarming degree. I say alarming because those waters are alive with piranhas, the small fishes that will eat the flesh right off the bones of any unfortunate living creature that falls prey to them.

Earthquakes and typhoons notwithstanding, this was the most frightening half-hour of my life! Carreras took a surprisingly practical view of the situation. As we headed frantically for the nearest landing place, he advised me calmly, "If the boat goes down, be sure to keep your gun above water so it won't rust."

Gaining safety, we found another boat and split up our party. Our destination was a ranch near the hamlet of Hayes. Sleepy inhabitants roused themselves from day-long siestas to provide us with a couple of ancient Ford cars, in which we made our bumpy way to the ranch. The *capataz* (foreman) was a handsome Guarani Indian. With him lived his wife and child and several female domestics. The women were very shy and I scarcely saw them during the several days I was there. The child was a toddler of about three, friendly with everyone. She had no toys of any kind, and when I found her playing lovingly with a dead partridge, I was so touched that, on my return to town, I sent her a huge Teddy bear.

The ranch house was adobe with mud floors. The beds were rough wooden frames with strips of rawhide woven across the frames and no sign of mattresses or covers. I did not have my clothes off during the whole time I was there.

During the day we went hunting. Among the hunters who went afoot with the pointer dogs was Carreras, who would walk miles without end but was afraid of horses. I elected to go horseback with the *capatax* and others and a strange assortment of Indian mongrel dogs. These dogs were accustomed to hunt for their own food, and shooting behind them was certainly an unorthodox experience. The system was to keep your eye on one particular dog. When his nose went down and his tail began to wag, you put spurs to your horse and galloped up as the dog raised the quail. The trick then was to get your horse to stand still long enough to take aim and shoot the bird and at the same time not shoot off the dog's head if he leaped into the air in the effort to bag your quarry. I galloped about all day and had a wonderful time, never shooting a thing, not even a dog.

During the afternoon we took our guns and walked through the nearby forest. Here the wildlife was so innocent that it did not even move off at our approach. Strange bright birds perched on branches within arm's reach, eying us curiously. Monkeys chattered at us with angry absurdity, without fear. No one cared to shoot such creatures as these. Only the *capataz* shot a monkey, under the mistaken impression that that was what we had come out for, but embarrassed by our glances of reproof, he shot no more.

The evenings were made turbulent by Indians encamped near-by. They had come down from the wilderness to sell pelts and, having sold them, stocked up on "fire water." From the ranch we could see their roaring fires, hear their wild songs. The *capataz* barred all windows and doors and would not allow us to show a light. It seemed like some grade-B movie. But by nightfall I was too tired to be agitated and always slept peacefully, rolled in my coat, without even taking off my boots.

Europe

The tremendous work and experience afforded me by that South American tour gave me my first real sense of being a recognized concert dancer. I felt artistically better armed, fortified to assimilate what lay ahead in new environments, to strengthen and extend my capacities.

Our North American equivalent of winter was just coming on in South America when we left by French liner for the Mediterranean. I had performed steadily for sixteen months. I now received a reward in the form of an unbrokenly beautiful voyage over the calm South Atlantic. Sea and sky were at peace. Blue days followed silver nights in an atmosphere of timelessness. It was as though our ship, like an explorer, had discovered a limbo of rest. Tensions fell away. I danced on the gently rolling deck with a rediscovered joy of dancing for its own sake, with the universe for a stage, the stars for an audience.

It was twenty days to Almería, Spain. My sister, as fiddle-footed as I when there was a prospect of travel, joined me in Almería. In Granada we spent some afternoons with Manuel de Falla in his walled garden. He was hard at work on a new opera but seemed quite happy to take time out to discuss with us his *Amor Brujo*. He explained to me how the ballet had been born and his concept of the ideal staging for it.

We found the great maestro to be small in physique, growing quietly old in years. He was gentle and courtly and his love for gypsy music and dance remained undiminished. His advice to us was to go to the *cuevas*, not as sightseers but with someone who was a friend of the gypsies. To this end he brought about a meeting with Murcillo Laborda, an old guitarist, said to have taught Segovia his first notes.

61

And so with Laborda we visited the *albaicin*. Though he was *busno*, he spoke Cale and knew everyone on the Sacred Mountain. Our opportunity was thus freed of the superficial, tourist aspect, but I do not imply that we were accepted as great friends of the gypsies. I doubt if any *busno* ever really knows these people, for instinctively theirs is a strangely hermetic nature.

However, they accepted us up to a point. They forgot us while they sang and danced, which was, in its way, important as well as sufficient. La Bisca, La Cagachina, La Paloma—I wonder what has become of them all. I can still see them outside the caves, posing self-consciously in their gaudy dresses for our cameras.

La Bisca did not dare tell any of the other gypsies, but she agreed to come down into town and dance for me. She defended doing this as teaching. Actually, she just danced, allowing me to follow along as best I could. She tried hard to answer my snowstorm of questions, but, of course, most gypsy knowledge of dance is sheer instinct.

In town Bisca appeared not unlike any flapper. Her curly red-gold hair was bobbed, her low-waisted cotton dress was knee-length, her stockings were rolled, but when she danced a farruca . . .! She had not dared bring a guitarist with her, so she danced to the playing of a half-blind accompanist who improvised on the wornout old piano in the all-night cafe where we had our rendezvous. Quickly she drew an audience. Sleepy heads popped from doorways along the balcony around the patio; passersby, halting in surprise, came in to join the *jaleo*. Caught up in the contagion of enthusiasm, I began to dance with her. Some tourists on their way to the Alhambra paused to watch and gave us each ten dollars!

I danced a concert in Granada that made my name known. Forthwith a young bullfighter, making his debut at seventeen, sent a member of his *cuadrilla* to ask if I would permit him to dedicate a bull to me on the following Sunday. With alacrity I accepted!

I sat in a box, his *capa de luz* draped across the front of it. And when he threw his hat to me in formal dedication, I was,

Carreras notwithstanding, in love with him, even though I had never set eyes on him before. Just to round out the drama of the occasion, the bull caught and flung him into the air. Naturally I screamed—without realizing it. Happily sustaining only a broken rib, the *torero* rose in a fury, killing the bull with such neatness and dispatch that he was awarded ears and tail. I kept the bull's smelly old tail for years, a memento of having once played Carmen in real life.

Even that queen of cities, Seville, was scarcely enough to erase beautiful Granada from my memory, though where else but in Seville will one find such clean, opalescent mornings, such gay, song-studded nights?

In Seville I came under the tutelage of the great Otero. In the morning I took private lessons; at night, class lessons.

There were, actually, two Oteros. Private lessons were conducted by young Otero, a nephew and star pupil of the great maestro who made dance history, and presided over by the "original" Otero.

In the morning we had a pianist; in the evening guitar and bandurria accompanied the many dances whereby, in true Spanish fashion, the student learned. Class students were working girls. Andalusian aristocracy, wishing to take lessons, summoned the maestro to its homes.

Although old Otero had retired from teaching in favor of his nephew, nothing could have kept him away from the lessons. He was fiercely against all change in the Spanish dance, feeling that the substitution of *taconeo* for *lazos* was no less than criminal. It was my almost unbelievable good fortune to learn from this last and greatest master of the classic school the popular dances of the nineteenth century before they passed.

I found it possible too to learn a great deal about Spanish dance just walking along the streets of Seville, for here was the race that had originated this greatest of western dance arts. Every Andalusian is a dancer in that his every movement has innate physical balance and beauty of line. To find proof one need look no further than at a *chulo* lighting a cigarette in the Calle della Sierpos or a *morena* expressively waving her fan.

Luckily the Seville Exposition was in full swing when we were there. Evenings after class we went to the little theaters to see the various dancers, both Andalusian and flamenco. The stages were very small, yet patterns and motions of the dance seemed magically scaled to them. The pit was crowded tightly with tables, occupied solely by men who drank as they watched. In the arc of boxes were the ladies, the tourists, and students of the dance like myself.

I seized the opportunity to have some costumes made in Seville. My *traje de cola*, literally "tailed dress," or woman's dress with a train, was made by the dressmaker who had always done Pastora Imperio's dresses. She made mine an exact copy of Pastora's favorite. One day I came home to find the hotel washwoman weeping over this costume, weeping for the glory of the great Pastora.

Sometimes I look back and wonder if the Andalusian newsboys still dance sevillanas in the streets. Do you still get the *piropo* on the Calle della Sierpos? Do you still hear castanets and guitars in the patios at dusk? Do Otero's girls still ride through the streets in open carriages, their organdy flounces a-flutter, their castanets chattering?

We went to French Morocco—destination Fez—to see the Moorish dance in its native background. Here not Scheherazade or even Morgiana, but Fatima, of Jewish ancestry, a longtime favorite dancer of the sultan, taught me. Between lessons this gay and witty woman led me through the alleys of the Jewish quarter to buy silks and jewellike costumes.

She engaged a 3-piece orchestra for the lessons. At my first lesson the three Arab musicians laughed. "They aren't really laughing at you," Fatima explained. "It's just that you're supposed to move your belly, and they observe that you haven't belly enough to move."

The Christmas of 1929 we spent in Florence. Carreras obtained a large studio in the Piazza Donatello near the English cemetery where the Brownings rest. We settled in to enlarge my repertoire and refresh my costumes. We engaged a very young, very eager pianist, Luigi Dallapiccola, now a very well known

Guido Carreras and La Meri in Norway, 1931.

composer, and we had long rehearsals together for my forth-coming engagements.

We broke in the new program with a performance in Florence in January. Then we were off for my formal debut in Vienna.

It was a frightening point along the road. Not only was Vienna the cultural summit of Europe; it was also the home of the editor of the *Neue Frei Presse*, Felix Cleve, Europe's premier authority on dance, drama, and motion pictures.

Our money was low. For the sake of face I was installed in a suite in the Grand Hotel, while Lilian, Carreras and Dallapiccola took the cheapest rooms in the wilds of the top floor. For dinner, while Lilian hid in my bathroom, I would order a Wiener schnitzel for one. When the waiter had gone, Lilian and I would make a meal for two out of it.

Everyone was most courteous to me. There were interviews, dinner parties, receptions. But the plain fact was that, like the rest of the world, Vienna had no confidence in artistry being inherent in any American. The most general conclusion was that I was a rich young eccentric dabbling in art.

Curiously enough, however, this attitude did not close the minds of the public. After my first performance Dr. Cleve and the lesser critics alike came out with fine reviews. In fact, Cleve gave me what remains to this day the finest and fairest review I have ever had. Its greatest value was that it taught me a great deal, for in it he let me see my flaws as well as the virtues of my performance.

We arrived in Berlin at a pyrotechnic time—the year when the ballet and its supporting press and the moderns and theirs were at each other's throats. As it happened, this worked out very well indeed for me. Paradoxically, my program, mixing both philosophies of movement, inspired both sides to roar that *this* was true dance in its purest form! For the time being, I took to the field of diplomacy, visiting local studios impartially, becoming friends too with Mary Wigman and observing her classes.

In Berlin we let face go by the board, all of us staying, as befitted our financial status, in the cheap rooms under the roof, those cubbyholes customarily occupied by the maids and chauffeurs of the rich guests. In no wise did it seem to harm us socially. While we found Berliners stern, they were invariably helpful. Our jaunts through the city must have been something of a nuisance to the natives, for Lilian and I spoke not a word of German. But we were never ignored and were helped with great patience.

I was engaged for Dance Week in Oslo. In view of my awed admiration for Pavlova when I was an adolescent back in Texas, this hardly seemed possible, for during Dance Week I gave the matinees and Pavlova and her company the evening performances!

I could scarcely believe that it was to be my good fortune to thus come in contact with the immortal Pavlova. At the opening of the week a big banquet was given for the performers. Pavlova and I sat opposite each other at the long, narrow table. I was struck dumb, but she was serenely gracious. She told me that she knew I was a specialist in the ethnic field. "I would like for you to give your candid opinion of my Mexican dances," she said, and she said it in a way that made me feel she was really anxious to have the opinion of a fellow artist.

I have often wondered why, in all the millions of words written about her, so little has been said of her insatiable interest in the ethnic dance arts. She not only learned but staged the dances of Mexico. It was she also who discovered Uday Shankar and played Radha opposite his Krishna. He has since told me that she often cried bitterly, because she felt she was so inept in mastering the true Indian style. She also learned and staged the dances of Japan and of Spain. Here, then, was no single-minded classicist. She saw all dances of the world as equally beautiful, equally worthy.

In answering this bewildering request for an opinion of her jarabe, I cannot remember now exactly what I said to her. I remember only that I discovered I could discuss dancing objectively and intelligently, and that I felt, perhaps for the first time, that I had ideas on the subject that were definite and my own.

I remember too that it was at this banquet that the last photograph of Pavlova was made. En route from Oslo to Hamburg she was stricken will the illness that killed her.

When we left Norway, it was in the light of a success so resounding that we carried away contracts for a big tour the following autumn. So Dallapiccola went back to Italy; Lilian returned to the States; Carreras and I went back to Paris to work on a new repertoire.

My modest solo concert at the Salle d'Iéna was followed by an engagement to take the title role in a drama called *Cassandre*. It would be unrealistic to assume I got the part because I spoke excellent French. My French was all but lamentable. I got the part because Cassandre was a mute and my mimic talents were judged equal to it. I was on the stage throughout the three acts. With the exception of making two sounds (a demoniac laugh on entering and another at the end when everyone but Electra and I were dead), my task was to mirror facially all the undercurrents of the old Greek story. Mimicry came comparatively easily to me, but how I practiced those wild laughs! The hotel was small and anything but soundproof. I am sure that all within earshot decided I was drunk or crazy and very possibly both.

We saw wonderful plays and concerts. La Argentina in her production of *El Amor Brujo*; Uday Shankar and his company, giving me my first sight of East Indian dancing. I could not know how much it would mean to my future, but I went away from the performance walking on air. What an excitingly beautiful art! What a matchless artist to communicate it!

I took my courage in my hands and introduced myself to this godlike dancer. I found him a simple and sympathetic human being. I entreated him to give me lessons. He insisted that he did not teach but invited me to his home on the outskirts of Paris. In their airy villa I met his charming companion artists, among whom was a small, large-eyed boy named Ravi. We settled down on the floor, Indian style, while Shankar explained to me a little of the vast lore of Indian dance. Finally he gave me some records and some books to study and told me that if I would make my own dances, he would correct them in lieu of lessons.

I haunted his rehearsals and performances and spent long, happy hours creating an Indian dance. I titled it *Lasyanatana*.

Twice Shankar worked with me in correcting it, and eventually I
had an authoritative Indian dance that remains with me to this
day.

For my second and impending tour of Norway we engaged a
piano team, Depiane and Rossi. These were stage names.
Depiane was Jacques Paul-Boncour, whose uncle was the well-
known French diplomat. Rossi was Mme. Denise Blottière. For
my assisting artist my manager engaged Tony Gregory, a young
modern dancer. In September 1930 we were off again for the
land of the Vikings.

It was a wonderful tour because Jacques, Denise, and Tony
were gay companions and we had a great deal of laughter and
none of the contretemps that can disturb a tour if anyone falls
out of humor.

In one town there was only one upright piano, and Denise and
Jacques were reduced to standing up and interlacing four hands
on the one keyboard for the entire performance. In another
town the curtain was a rolled affair controlled by a very heavy
weight. At the conclusion of my first number Carreras leaped at
the curtain to bring it down fast. We heard "Bravo! Bravo!
Bravo!" with enthusiastic handclapping. Up went the curtain, I
took another bow, the curtain came down on more shouts of
"Bravo!" I took nine bows before we discovered that what we
thought were bravos was the groaning of that antiquated curtain.

Some towns afforded only one large dressing room, which *per
forza*, we all shared. I shall never forget the effect on an autograph hunter when our tall, bony Jacques, attired at the moment
in the chic of shorts, shoes, and socks, starched dickey and a
monocle, answered the knock on the door.

We went wearily down to the station at another town to
catch the midnight train. Many people were in the waiting
room, but no one paid any attention to us for the hour of our
wait. When the train came in at long last and we went out to
board it, all the people who had been waiting came out on the
platform and, as the train pulled out, cried, "Viva La Meri!"
Smiling cordially, they turned to go back to their homes.

Once more in Paris we resumed our strict daily routine of

rehearsals and preparation for appearances in Brussels and a tour
of southern France. Previous commitments now made it possible
for Tony to tour with us during the winter.

During our stay in Vienna I had been overwhelmed with the
enthusiasm of a handsome six-foot youngster, the son of Hendrik
van Loon. The boy had been writing to me steadily, and
from time to time I answered. I wrote him now, mentioning
that Carreras was looking for another male dancer. Two days
later William arrived, bag and baggage, to audition for the job!
He got it—perhaps as much for his gambler's courage as for his
ability.

In Brussels the entire court was to have been present for my
debut in February 1931. Just before my arrival the Queen
Mother died and the court went into mourning. I apparently
did not bring luck to rulers. During my engagement in Lima
they put the President in jail. In Spain the King took flight
from a revolution. I could not foresee it then, but in England
the King was to die.

Again in Paris in the spring another Paris concert. This time
Jacques Hebertot presented me at the Théâtre des Champs-
Élysées. It was a very chic affair. The theater itself is most
beautiful and has a tremendous reputation artistically. With my
audience glittering in full evening regalia, the whole atmosphere
was that of the golden age of the theater.

There was a great international fair in Paris that year, so for
the ethnic section of my concert, Carreras engaged several native
orchestras who appeared onstage with me. Generally, there was
little problem in this, for a couple of rehearsals set up the Mexican
orquesta típica, the flamenco guitarist, and the Hawaiian
strings and singers. But the Arabic musicians were another
matter. They refused to give me even a run-through.

"Why rehearse?" said the leader. "You give us the timing.
You dance and we play. When you stop, we stop."

And that's the way it was. I can assure you that I found it
very nerve-racking.

In June of 1931 Carreras and I found ourselves with a few
weeks off, so we popped over to London and got married. The

ceremony took place in a dingy mid-Victorian registry presided over by a beaming, if rather seedy-looking, civil clerk. However, glamour was provided by our two witnesses, Mr. Lord of the American consulate and the long-famous dancer, Maude Allan.

We went from London directly to Italy, taking a cottage in a tiny Tuscan village called I Ronchi. Happy to be back among Italians again, my husband spent most of his time with the local menfolk while I turned to my typewriter and wrote my first full-length book on dancing, *Dance as an Art-Form.*

We moved with the autumn to Florence, where Carreras placed me on the faculty of the state-subventioned Regis Academia dei Fidenti. There I held classes, staged ballets, and occupied myself quite happily. Teaching Italian girls presented certain problems, for although they were generally graceful, chic, and very musical, they were subject to last-minute withdrawals from productions under pressure of sudden disapproval from grand-mothers or fiancés. In some ways I found my evening classes, given gratis to working girls, more satisfying.

There was a tremendous reservoir of enthusiastic creative talent in the Academia. Young painters who did scenic and costume design, young writers who wrote plays, young musicians who would slave and turn out compositions over a weekend. It was exciting to work with such a wealth of talent at one's disposal.

For the first *Maggio Musicale Fiorentino* I was asked to stage an evening of dance, as much as possible using music by the composers who were to be guests of honor. It was quite an assignment, for however eager and talented my students were, they were far from professional. But we went to work with great will.

On performance night, among other works we presented a ballet to Respighi's *Poema Autumnale.* Maestro Respighi himself came back after the performance to praise us and to suggest cuts in his music to make it conform better to the dancing. Many a lesser artist would not have been so modest! On that night, too, I danced my first East Indian composition, to the intense gratification of the Indian composer who was present.

When the Fidenti closed for the summer, we went down to

the sea again, this time to Viareggio. Because we had invited
two young artists along, I found myself happily surrounded by
young people, with whom I could swim, sail, and play tennis.
Carreras went daily to the trap-shooting range. He bought me a
small shotgun and urged me to join him. Since I was the only
woman present, I became quite the darling of the group, which
included both prince and peasant. I am nearly blind in my right
eye, so I shoot, somewhat awkwardly, from my left shoulder.
When the day we were to shoot for prizes rolled around, everyone was very hopeful that I would win something. I took my
place and aimed carefully at the rim of the sand-bagged trench,
behind which crouched the man who operated the trap. When
the clay pigeon flew out, I was to track it and pull the trigger.

Anxious for me to win, the attendant made a hasty adjust-
ment of the machine so the clay pigeon would fly more slowly.
Like myself, he was overexcited. The bird lumbered up with all
the speed of an overfed Thanksgiving turkey to a height of some
four feet, whereupon it collapsed to the ground. Blasting away,
I hit the top of the sandbags, bringing the poor man gasping to
his feet. He had sought to help me and, for his trouble, had
eyes, ears, nose, and mouth filled with sand. "O, Signora!" he
chided me through sand-covered teeth. A miracle of self-control!

Thus did I become acquainted with Averardo, who worked
with us for fifteen years.

Back in Florence in the fall I was again active at the Fidenti
and made flying trips for solo concerts in the major Italian cities.
On one occasion I and my group of dancers were presented as
soloists with the Florentine Symphony Orchestra at a concert
given in the Uffizi Galleries. For the occasion I had built a
group composition with a percussive accompaniment on four
timpani. During the performance the timpanist came to my
dressing room to convey the unhappy information that one of
the drumheads had broken and he could not play.

"*Va bene*," I muttered, getting into my next costume.

I finished my North Indian solo, made my bows, then, climbing in through the orchestra, complete with clanking bracelets
and flowing *chador*, I played the timpani for my girls. I learned

in passing that nothing is more fun than wacking three large timpani! When one receives an accolade of applause from the Florentine Symphony Orchestra for the doing, it's even better.

Carreras wanted a home in the country. With this end in view he talked endlessly to his friends and made numerous trips out of town. But nothing he saw entirely pleased him, so when the Fidenti closed for the summer, we bought bicycles and set out on a leisurely trip along the Tuscan coast in search of a home. Some seven miles south of Leghorn, darkness caught us on the road. We rang the bell at a huge iron gate on the Via Aurelia and peasants within agreed to put us up for the night. Four rows of great pines and a high stone wall were between the house and the motor road. Low, thick live oaks were between the house and the bouldered drop to the sea.

After a robust supper Carreras and I walked through the trees and looked down on the sea, ruffled by a gentle wind as it dreamed under the full moon. Fireflies sequined the foliage and nightingales sang. Before we went to sleep, we knew we had found our home.

As soon as we moved in, we contracted with workmen to build a huge studio, a hundred square feet in space, in which I could dance and work. We sent for Averardo, who dropped everything and came flying (on bicycle) to help us. The months sped by happily, spent in refurbishing, painting, and gardening; after all, the fascination of a country home is that it is never, never finished.

The year was filled with many homely, bucolic joys. There was hunting in the fall and swimming from May to December. Lilian and Dave came to visit us for a month, and we had many other visitors for a day, a week, a month—my dear friend Mimma, my lovely ex-pupil Laura, the Misses Garibaldi. The American consul entertained the officers of an American destroyer in our home, and a friend in the Italian navy brought his submarine practically to our doorstep. There were picnics in the hills and below the ancient Roman bridge. There was a Christmas with American touches—a tree and open house. And my beloved spaniel, Booch, presented me with a half dozen fat puppies.

There was dancing too. I held summer courses and presented an outdoor festival in the nearby gardens of the Castello Birindelli. Best of all, the Vienna Dance Congress invited me to join them, representing Italy.

Not choosing to go on this trip, Carreras allowed me to go alone. I felt very small indeed, all by myself in wonderful, romantic Vienna. I couldn't speak a word of German and my French left much to be desired. But everyone was kind, everyone was hospitable, and there were laughter and song under the lindens and down the galleries.

I sat on a large jury, helping to judge winners of both solo and group choreographic works, offered by dancers from all over Europe. Beautiful—and so anxious—these aspiring young people streamed across the stage of the concert hall in a kaleidoscopic sequence of ballet, modern, and neo-ethnic.

In the late afternoons we went out to the park to sit at an outdoor table, sip a glass of beer and watch the folk groups from Holland, Hungary, Czechoslovakia, and many other countries perform their colorful national dances.

Only two concerts were given in the great concert hall during the congress. The first was by Grete Wiesenthal, darling of Vienna and one of the most inspiring dancers I have ever seen. She moved as though the music were flowing from her own lovely body, and she danced in the very sun of living joy.

The second concert in the great hall was mine. The congress had asked me to present a program of dances from those countries that had not sent representatives. It was my first all-ethnic performance, and I was received with a warmth I was never to forget. Somehow the director of the stage crew, gray-haired and rubicund, managed to interpret my talk of cues and lighting to his smilingly sympathetic henchmen. Given the greenroom in which to dress, I seemed, in its austere quiet, to hear the beating of my own excited heart. I felt oriented by the sight of my familiar costumes and the soft, sweet pungency of grease paint. When the curtains of heavy scarlet parted, no Carreras was behind the spotlights, no Averardo was there to control the sound installation with his sure hand. But the crewmen wished me luck in

the murmured equivalent of "Break your leg!" and I stepped onto the glowing stage—straight into the deepest emotional success
of my career.

How an artist feels, with quivering antennae of the heart, the
waves that sweep across the footlights from the audience! Before the first dance was half performed, Vienna and I were in
love, as, ideally, audience and artist can be. In the warm sea of
this love I could have danced forever. Closing with the Spanish
dance *Intermezzo* from Granados's *Goyescas*, I repeated the
dance three times, for my lover-audience had hurled itself up to
the footlights and, leaning toward me across their lambent fire,
beat the rim of the stage with their fists, demanding encores. At
last I had to come forward to tell them, *"Die program ist sehr
schnell. Ich bin kaput. Aber ich liebe dich!"* They understood
my almost indecipherable German for the declaration it was and,
with applause and laughter, let me go, although several climbed
up over the footlights and carried away as mementos one small
comb and some madronos that had fallen from my costumes.

After my performance, still moving in a dream, I went with
Fraulein Wiesenthal's party to a nearby rathskeller for refresh-
ments. As we entered, all the people in the room stood up from
their tables, clapping and shouting "Bravo! Bravo!", while in my
honor the dance orchestra swung into "El Relicario."

But no artist in our party was forgotten that night. As I sat
at the table receiving homage from a procession of strangers, the
musicians played "The Blue Danube" and, to the applause of the
watchers, Grete Wiesenthal waltzed with a partner. Scarcely had
she seated herself when the music went into "Un bel di" from
Madame Butterfly for the Japanese gentleman in our party. And
then into a czardas to honor the Hungarian winner of the congress's first prize. Grete Wiesenthal said our whole party must
join in this rousing dance. The Japanese, elegant in his white
tabi, was my partner and, to the mixture of gentle laughter and
cheers of our informal audience, we did what we could for the
czardas.

After that triumph it seemed difficult to return to the bucolic
life. Even the deep peace I have always found in the beauty

of nature seemed too gentle to subdue my hunger to return to
the siren theater.

However, Carreras, twenty-five years my senior and with forty
years of traveling behind him, longed to settle down in a home
and be done with wandering. As obedient artist and faithful
wife, I acquiesced. Nevertheless, I spent many hours staring
through tear-dimmed eyes at the sea, weeping for the Orient I
might never see.

Sensing my unspoken restlessness, Carreras accepted offers for
concerts in Italy and certain special performances in Rome.

The first of these calls to the Eternal City was at the invitation of the Princess San Faustino. She was a beautiful and dynamic woman in her seventies. Tall, slender with snow-white
hair, she seemed to me everything a fairy-tale princess would be.
During the day she dressed all in black with fabulous pearls; in
the evenings, all in white with diamonds.

Arriving in the capital, I was summoned to her palace for a
late-morning appointment. Ushered into her rococo bedroom, I
found her sitting regally in a satin-sheeted bed, a lap desk across
her knees. Her velvet bed jacket was edged in ermine; her white
hair was impeccably dressed. Besides myself, a dozen persons
were present; some of them were her secretaries, some were
gentlemen of nobility, and all were jumping to do her bidding.
The ivory telephone by her bed rang incessantly; from their
trend I got the impression that her sharp demands fell impartially on king and dictator. A princess to the palace born—and born
in Chicago, U.S.A.

She was staging a great benefit, the *Triumfo del Grano*, a production in which she was involving all the society and talent of
Rome. She informed me that I was both choreographer and
soloist. I was to find that she stood unequivocally behind me in
every detail.

On the night of the performance she invited me to join her in
her box after my part in the program was finished. As I sat
with her a handsome, towering man entered to pay his respects—
the infante of Spain! To my shame be it said that Emily Post
failed me, or rather I failed Emily Post! Not certain whether I

should stand for royalty or, being a lady, should sit, I sat. The princess sensed my dilemma. Without turning her head, she exclaimed testily, "Sit still, darling; he's only a prince. *You* are a creative artist."

The second time I was called to Rome it was again in the capacity of choreographer-soloist, this time for the splendid project of a week's performance of *Quo Vadis*. Dreamed up as a tourist attraction, it was to be done in sequence and on the very spots where historically each episode had taken place. The musical score had been commissioned; the Pope's permission to remove the cross from the Coliseum had been obtained. Even the lions had been hired. To this mammoth daytime entertainment there were to be added evening performances in the Villa Borghese Park of ballets by Italian composers. Days passed in endless discussion of details.

And then, at what seemed the very last moment, the government decided to spend all its money on a campaign in Abyssinia. It would have done better to stick to *Quo Vadis*!

It was not ordained that I should live out my days in a villa by the Mediterranean Sea. With an innate desire to be "up and at 'em," I welcomed the wolf that came snuffling at our door and forced Carreras to put away his shotgun and dust off his spotlights. The wolf was my ally, pushing my return to deadline rehearsals and the welcome fever of costume creation.

We went to England, Carreras, Averardo, and I. It was January of 1936 and we were under contract to the august L. G. Sharpe, manager of many great stars. I knew that he had handled Paderewski since his debut. Reasoning that this made Mr. Sharpe a gentleman of considerable years, I was surprised to be met at the boat by a Britisher not only handsome but young. We were halfway to London before I grasped that this was not L. G. Sharpe but his representative, Cameron Stockwell. Soon he became Stocky and my lifelong friend.

We opened for a week's performance at a small art theater. Back in my dressing room, wearing my costume for the *White Peacock*, I waited for the curtain-up warning bell. Earnestly my face looked back at me from the globe-lit mirror. I had

returned—returned to that wonderful world of international
touring. I was in London, that great city that, once it declared
its love for an artist, would remain faithful to the end. This was
no ordinary concert I was giving. This evening's work was a
Rubicon to cross. The butterflies in my stomach metamorphosed
into hummingbirds. Calling faintly for help, I lay down on the
floor in my spanking-white costume. Stocky rushed out for
some pills for me to swallow, and when the warning bell
sounded, I was ready in the wings.

For the opening the house had been papered partially with
celebrities. The audience was not exactly Vienna. This was
England, and the English are not hasty in giving their love. But
when the program was over, a lovely gray-haired lady approached
the box office firmly and, over all protests, insisted on paying
for her ticket. "It is too beautiful a concert to be seen gratis,"
she declared reprovingly. "I *will* pay!" She turned out to be
John Galsworthy's sister, and she attended every performance
I gave. Thus making my first English allies, I began to feel that
I could conquer all Britain!

Before my first week was over, I had been engaged for two
weeks, sixteen performances, at the chic Savoy Theatre. Between engagements I busied myself with varied activities. I gave
a conference on Indian dancing for the Indian Society; I danced
in a hospital for child charity cases; I created a new dance and
had the costume made for it. From a handsome Coldstream
Guardsman I took lessons in Irish dancing. In the great ballroom of the hotel we put a bottle of Chianti on one end of the
marble mantel and a bottle of Irish whisky on the other end . . .
and I learned a good deal about both the Irish and Irish dancing.

I also tried my best to study Scottish dancing with a soldier
of the Black Watch. But here I met with the one absolute re-
buff of my whole career.

"Tis no dance for a woman," he informed me dourly, and no
sort of persuasion would move him. I could not insist too much.
Having seen the flings and reels as done by the Black Watch, I
knew he was all too right—that truly it was "no dance for a
woman"—for a wilder, more athletic performance I have never

seen. So mostly Scottish me has no fling in my repertoire to this day, no Allen tartan among my costumes.

Lady Ravensdale interested herself in my Savoy performances and promised that the court would attend my opening. But before it could take place, the empire was plunged in gloom by the sudden death of George V; tragic and profoundly impressive was the funeral cortege, passing Marble Arch beneath our hotel windows.

For ordinary people life went on its ordinary way. I opened on the scheduled date and many titled persons attended, unofficially. The physical work of giving eight solo shows a week was grueling yet filled with satisfactions. Dame Adeline Genée wrote me a charming note of congratulation. Arnold Haskell printed his approval of my *Bolero, 1860* on point. After a performance the enthusiastic president of the Folk Dance Society threw himself at my none-too-clean bare feet. Queen Mary's own prebendary attended my performances, gave his approval to even my wildest dances, and repaid me by taking me through closed Buckingham Palace.

At the end of my run Stocky announced that I was to audition for an Australian impresario with a view to a tour in Australasia. This opportunity, like the silent swinging open of a huge door, disclosed a long vista of exotic beauty: India, Java, China, Japan, and, at the end, Australasia. Could I step across the threshold, enter this enchanted realm? So much hung on this audition that I was a jelly of nerves! I pictured this redoubtable Australian impresario as a tall, white-haired combination of Gordon Craig and David Belasco.

When I stepped onstage to dance for him, I could not discern him in the darkened auditorium. After it was all over and the contract signed, sealed, and delivered, I met this frightening A. D. M. Longden. Good gracious! He was of medium height, very slight in build, and surely on the sunny side of thirty. His overlarge overcoat hung loosely on his thin frame, and his enormous dark eyes seemed to look upon the world with the diffident surprise of Walt Disney's beloved dwarf, Dopey!

Appearances are deceptive. A. D. M. Longden was an inspired dynamo, as he amply proved when he took me to Australia.

Australasia

We embarked at Genoa for Australasia. On that very day, May 5, 1936, indeed at the very hour we stepped aboard the Italian Line S.S. *Romolo*, airplanes roared over the port and city dropping clouds of colored-paper squares announcing the *adunata*, Italy's victory over Abyssinia.

We were joined at Naples by Mario Salerno, our old friend, who was to play for me on this tour. Laura Mollica was going along as my assistant, and we picked her up at Messina. This, with Averardo, Carreras, and myself, was our little company of five. For thirty-eight long days our home was the *Romolo*. The first time we left her after Messina was Cochin, India, on May 23. In my logbook Cochin takes its place for fascination alongside exotic Fez.

A quick tropical shower had cooled the air. Each one in our party of nine had his own rickshaw. Though the town was somewhat primitive, it was also surprisingly clean, even with cows and dogs roaming at will through the streets and narrow lanes of the bazaars.

We stopped to see the interior of a Jewish synagogue, and a group of Indian ladies, bright as flowers in varicolored saris, invited us to attend a conference on religion just starting in a pavilion across the way.

Of course we accepted. We couldn't understand a word the expositors were saying but were deeply interested in the various schools of thought represented on the platform and in the audience. It was reassuring to see Buddhist and Christian, Mohammedan and Hebrew in full good temper discussing contrasting points of their faiths. The pavilion was crowded to capacity with old and young, even crawling babies, and all were quiet and attentive.

At Colombo, Ceylon (now Sri Lanka), we were met at the dock by the music critic of the town's largest newspaper and the manager who was to book us in India. We had only three hours. Docking at nine, we had to be aboard again by noon. I wanted to rush ashore and see and see and see! If only I were an ordinary tourist, free to absorb Colombo at leisure!

First we had to go to the newspaper offices to have our pictures taken—no such luxury as their coming to us—and this formality used up an hour. We rushed to take a car and see the city, but it seemed we could have only an hour for that, for we must go and call on a newspaper editor, who proceeded to convoy us to a thoroughly American hotel for a thoroughly American cocktail. Of course, I reflected, I wouldn't be there at all were it not that I was an artist. Still, if for just that short three hours . . .

On shipboard I practiced long hours every day but with a peculiar sense of confinement, and I began to grow heartily tired of it. On June 5 my spirits lifted—we arrived in Fremantle.

Since it was the Australian winter, the air was cool yet marvelously invigorating. This time we received a bonus—eight hours in port instead of three. Four reporters met us, plus a charming married couple, come to show us about. We drove in a big car from Fremantle to Perth, had four interviews and a fine luncheon, and were delivered back on board practically hidden under flowers. We couldn't decently find any fault with our first taste of Australia.

Five days later, Melbourne. Three reporters, two photographers, luncheon on board, on to the hotel. Bathe and change? Nonsense, the press had arrived! Nine interviews—separately— that first day. Probably I should have reveled in it, but I did not. When it came to the glamour part, I felt woefully deficient. The only part of a tour I really liked was the work of preparation and the performances themselves. But it did touch me that the Melbourne dancing teachers welcomed me with flowers and hospitable telegrams.

There are differences between getting back in shape after an interval on land and one at sea. I don't know whether the long stay at sea made me clumsy—it could probably have happened anyway—but in rehearsal I acquired a bad canvas burn on one knee and knocked the nail off a big toe, making it necessary to skip point work. As a result, within a week I had to make some new dances and the costumes to go with them.

Rehearsals were endless and hectic. We had engaged a violinist and cellist to join Mario in my accompaniments and to play interludes between dances.

Mr. Longden had become frightened to death at his temerity in bringing a solo dance concert to Australia, which had seen no dancing save pure ballet since Maude Allan had danced there in 1911. But our debut on June 20 was very successful, and I was as glad for Mr. Longden as for us. We were booked for eight concerts in Melbourne and ended by giving twenty-two—eight performances a week. I performed more than sixty different dances during the engagement and was greatly excited to discover that many people bought season tickets and sat in the same seat for every performance.

Here too I learned something about what might wryly be called the fringe benefits of such success. We were inundated with invitations. I could plead the discipline of work to get out of many parties, but not the official ones. It was less fun than you would think, entering a large ballroom to strains of a triumphal march, with the dancing stopped to permit those present to goggle. Less fun than it might seem, dancing with oldsters for the sole and simple reason that they were *Sir* Somebody, or sitting as Exhibit A in the honor seat with all lesser mortals a good city block away!

Mornings were marked off for three-hour rehearsals. I had to look high and low to find time to shampoo my hair and manicure my nails. At one performance I dislocated an ankle but finished the show, having the ankle yanked back into place and taped up the next morning.

On my one day off, when there was no performance, I danced for hours in order that sketch artists could catch me in movement. In the rain I went to the local park to be photographed with peacocks, because my *White Peacock* dance was being greatly acclaimed.

We wound up the Melbourne stay with a dash of romance. Laura and Mario, succumbing to the down-under moon, had fallen in love. They cabled Laura's mother for permission to marry and received it in time to be married there. Closing our season July 11, we went to the cathedral bright and early the next morning for the ceremony. Imagine our surprise when we found three thousand people crowded around the church. Even with the willing help of mounted police it took us fifteen minutes to move about a hundred yards. People cheered and threw flowers and held their babies aloft to get a look at us. After the ceremony we made a round of parties given for the bride and groom by the Italian colony. At every house toasts were many and flowery. Not before or since have I drunk so many kinds of wine in one evening.

After two concerts in Geelong came the formidable task of spreading out costumes to be stamped by the customs officials. Having learned their predilection for stamping everything, but everything—from Spanish shawls to American panties—I had made a regular practice of handling the costumes myself, to make it as easy as possible for them.

In these times when people travel everywhere by air, I often wonder how artists recoup their energies. I would never have survived my tours if it hadn't been for the periodic sea journeys that enabled me to recuperate. At the time of which I am writing not even the notoriously inhospitable Tasman Sea could stir me from my berth during the three-day trip to New Zealand.

In Wellington the whole merry-go-round started again. I danced my heart out in concert after concert, autographed hundreds of photographs, gave hundreds of interviews. Proud mamas from all over the country brought talented children to dance for me. Every mail brought bushel baskets of fan letters, even from girls on remote farms who had never seen me dance.

My teeth began to give me trouble, and I couldn't stay in one place long enough to have anything done about them.

Christchurch, Dunedin, Oamaru, Palmerston, Auckland—speeches, social obligations, nightly performances. A wide gray streak appeared in my hair, and I began wearing coronet braids to cover it up.

In Auckland, on an August night, I was on the way to the theater for the fifty-seventh concert of our Australian tour. It seemed the right moment to say to Mr. Longden, "If I were the captain of my soul, I wouldn't be doing this performance tonight. I'm dead beat. Lately I've been drawing mental blanks in the middle of my oldest dances."

"I see," he said.

I threw myself around the stage for ten numbers without really having energy enough to control my overtired muscles. At the outset of the eleventh number I started a perfectly simple little run across the stage. I heard a snap, like the breaking of a bass-viol string, and found I had no control over my right leg. I paused a second to cover it, thinking it was a passing cramp. But it wasn't. I signaled for the curtain to be lowered. Panic overwhelmed me. I burst into tears. Carreras carried me into the dressing room. Mr. Longden cried, "I'll tell the people the performance is over and to get their money from the box office."

Our Australian electrician kept his head and had a better idea. He ordered the trio onstage to finish the show. I have never understood how, amid the welter of doctors running in and out and my lamentations rising to a crescendo on the strength of whisky restoratives, but Mario, Joan, and Tom brought the program to an orderly finish with a lovely chamber-music group.

"A torn muscle, madam," announced two doctors and taped me up. Back in the hotel I took two sleeping pills and launched into a spirited night-long colloquy with Lilian, Mother, and even Pappy.

In the morning my eyes had the appearance of two dissipated oysters on the half shell, but, ignoring this, the doctors said, "Tomorrow, madam, you may walk, but very carefully. You may not dance for three weeks."

And what of our company, which must be housed and paid? We decided at least to push on to Rotorua for rest and treatments for my injured leg.

Rotorua is a health resort where people go for the sulfur
baths. My spirits revived under morning treatments. As soon as
I finished, I would catch the bus for Wakawarewarewa, and soon
all the Maoris knew me, bless their hospitable, gentle hearts!

The Maoris are a Polynesian people of Aryan blood with that
culture of gentleness that only long generations of high ideals
can give a race. They are darkly beautiful and possessed of a
rare sense of rhythm and harmony. They are never cross, always
laughing, and tremendously sympathetic and understanding.

Guide Bella (aged seventy but appearing fifty and dancing like
twenty) taught me the poi dances and something of the hakas.
Princess Rangi, who had us to native meals of giant mussels
boiled in the natural hot springs, organized dances for us. But
my particular friend was Meri, because our names were the same.
And what does *meri* mean in Maori? Battle-ax!

I wanted to buy a costume. I have never met more unvenal
people in all my travels. They would not sell me a costume—
they *gave* it to me.

I didn't wait around any three weeks for my leg to heal. Ten
days after the accident I made up an easy program and began
again, on a tour of North Island. This time we took a big nine-
passenger car and a truck for the material. It was nicer than
train travel, for we took along picnic lunches and ate in the open
air. In three widely separated towns—Hamilton, Hastings, and
Gisborne—we gave six concerts in eight days. It took a bit of
doing, but we were amply rewarded by the appreciative audiences.

The moment we were back in Rotorua I telephoned Princess
Rangi, asking her to invite all my Maori friends to the *whare-
matoro* (meetinghouse) that evening. Wanting to return their
hospitality, I gave them a program of dances that were mile-
stones on the fabled Maori westward migration—India, Spain,
Morocco, North America, Mexico, Peru, and Hawaii.

Never has there been such an audience. From small children
to ninety-year-olds, they were breathlessly attentive. Even a lift
of my eyebrow was observed and understood. At the end of
each number they fairly squealed with delight. Drunk with their
appreciation, I danced better than ever before in my life.

They, in their enthusiasm, turned the tables and danced for me—old rituals that no pakeha (white person) had seen since Edward VIII passed through as Prince of Wales. We ended the evening by all dancing together and very nearly not getting home to bed. At the last we climbed the path to watch the big geyset spouting hundreds of feet of spray into the moonlit night.

And all this had come about as a consequence of an injured leg!

There was an audience of several thousand in the town hall for our farewell appearance in Auckland. For the first time I wore the Spanish costumes I had been making in my few spare hours on the road. "Olé!" cried members of the small Spanish colony. "Viva España!"

Besides thirty-six hectic hours with interviewers and photographers, Sydney afforded us the task of repacking all our personal belongings. We were leaving winter behind for a while and must have our summer clothes ready.

Our next stop being Brisbane, Queensland, I crawled into my berth almost before the last camera shutter had clicked. Perhaps eleven hours' sleep should have been enough, but I was woefully annoyed when the train conductor, all courtesy, woke me at seven with a cup of steaming tea! However, the country on which I looked as I sipped my tea was lovely; the sun and warmth were delicious. I may be a Kentuckian by birth, but I am forever San Antonio by climate.

There were few if any towns between Sydney and Brisbane. Whenever we passed a lonely little shack, inhabitants would come running out to wave at the train and clamor for newspapers to be thrown to them. I always wondered how impressed they were by "all the news that's fit to print" in my somewhat outdated issues of the *New York Times*.

No stop was without its troublesome backstage incident, yet things were always happening to touch my heart too and take the anger out of me.

In Brisbane it was the arrival backstage of a five-year-old child who looked like a Lippi angel. She swept me a low curtsy and said, "I thank you very much. I enjoyed every minute of it."

Will you please accept this little gift?" As she surrendered her small package to me, her face broke into an impish smile and she confided, "It's a tickly powder puff!"

The next morning, without enthusiasm from me, we got up at four to go out for a shoot. That enthusiastic hunter, my husband, wouldn't go without me. I shot nothing, just trudged around the countryside, my shotgun in the crook of my arm, my body gratefully accepting the warm sunshine.

In Brisbane I took part in perhaps the most stylized soiree of my experience. The Dancing Teachers Association gave me a banquet. I was seated next to the governor's wife, Lady Blair, and had my turn at making a speech. Then I was seated at a different "special" table, and people were brought up by twos to sit across from me and talk for precisely three minutes each. I was tempted to talk longer to many—not just because they were interesting, but to see what would happen!—but the thing was so delicately balanced that the next couple were often slid into their chairs in the middle of a sentence addressed to or by a departing couple.

It seemed to me that my offstage hours were even more active than those onstage. Local celebrities, local flora and fauna—I was photographed with them all, including the peacocks, wallabies, and koala bears. Laura had to do my shopping, because a barricade of autograph seekers prevented me setting foot in any shop. And I auditioned hopeful students.

What can one ever say to these many "talented" children? They gaze, wide-eyed and doubtful, when one tries to explain that talent, even technique, are never enough for success. Stamina, love, single-mindedness, knowledge, musicality, emotion, dedication—when one possesses these, there is still something one must understand and master—the art of bowing!

I always knew what they were thinking. "She exaggerates. Any girl who has pretty legs and can pirouette can become a second Pavlova!" One reason I was the last person on earth entitled to tell them this was a mistake was that, fifteen years earlier, I had exactly the same idea! How, then, could I question that they too might start out with it and come as far as I had, indeed very possibly go farther?

I am sure the auditions were unsatisfactory to us all, for I could only give them a kernel of advice, difficult for them to accept, and try to guess if in their characters there was enough of that priceless ingredient—the will to do—to make it worthwhile for them to start the long, hard struggle.

When we left Brisbane for Rockhampton, my little Lippi angel came to the train to see me off and presented me with—a box of silkworms! "And if you feed them," she assured me gravely, "they will make the silk for your costumes."

Rockhampton sits right smack on the Tropic of Capricorn and is about as hot as you would suppose it might be. In such heat the men in Cuba or Argentina or Texas would be coatless in the daytime and very likely even at dinner. Not so the British. All the men wore dark jackets, stiff collars, and ties and, in the evenings, black dinner jackets. I decided that the real "white man's burden" was the collar and tie.

In Sydney I found a tremendous interest in Spanish dancing, coupled with a complete ignorance of what it was. Backstage visitors and fan letters asked me so many questions that I decided to give a free concert in the theater and invite teachers and dancers. It created such a stir that I gave private lessons eight hours a day for two days following my engagement.

We did three one-night stands on the way to Melbourne—Goulburn, Wagga Wagga, and Wangaratta—and in one of the towns the audience, seeing a live show for the first time and being accustomed to movies, brought along bags of peanuts to munch. I have no excuse for my reaction to this innocently ignorant behavior save that I was bone-tired, but during my *White Peacock* dance I stopped Mario's accompaniment, stepped to the footlights, and informed the audience that if it couldn't stop munching, I couldn't dance. The poor things were so flabbergasted that thereafter they scarcely dared applaud. The next morning, while we were packing, a lady called. She had walked three miles into town just to tell us how much she had enjoyed the performance.

Our company split up in Melbourne. The Salernos left for Italy. Mr. Longden, whom I had come to love devotedly, sailed for India as our advance man. We bade good-bye to our Australian musicians, Joan and Tom. Like the Ten Little Indians, now we were three—Carreras, Averardo, and I. From here on we would do our concertizing with recorded music. It was the first time I had ever been without live musicians. But ever since my debut concert in New York, I had used recordings for typical music of the Orient, Polynesia, and, in some instances, South America. Lilian had found and shipped me dozens of recordings from the States, and with these I had built up my repertoire during my on-the-road rehearsals.

We three sailed for Tasmania. I slept for eighteen hours, unaware of the boat's pitching across a waterway justifiably considered worse than the English Channel at its worst.

It was important to me that the concerts in Tasmania, in Launceston and Hobart, go well, because they were my first with the canned music. At Hobart we were rescued from a dilemma. We found I was to appear in a concert hall that was without battens or ropes to hang our curtains. Just when we thought all was lost, the manager of a traveling burlesque show arrived with his stagehands, and they worked all day out of sheer kindness of heart, rigging up a stage for us.

We began collecting ourselves to move on to India. There were more recordings to buy, clothes and costumes to clean, equipment to condition—all those thousand and one things one never finds time to do in the course of traveling and performing.

This time in Melbourne we were received almost like old acquaintances. Invitations were on a more *intime* basis, and we savored the lack of strain. However, on one occasion things did not go so well.

Knowing that my mother was of Scottish descent, a very charming Scottish couple invited us to dinner. We were met at their palatial gate by a piper in kilts and tartan who piped us up the drive. When, after cocktails, we went in to dinner, we found the baronial dining hall decorated with claymores, tartan, and dour family portraits.

I loved it all—right through the soup.

Then the piper piped in the main course—the haggis. Three

times around the table he went skirling, followed by the butler bearing the steaming dish.

I had heard of haggis (as who has not), but I had no idea what it was. It is the stomach of a sheep, stuffed with some sort of cereal!

I was just not Scottish enough. In the midst of all the ceremony I turned an odd shade of green and excused myself from the table.

Five months, one hundred eight concerts. At twelve to sixteen solos per program, it adds up. I suspected then what I now know, that it was the most glamorous tour I ever had. More personal adulation than I would have thought possible; kindness, compliments, flowers. I was painted, sculptured, and photographed endlessly. A racehorse, a hat style, a popular sundae were named La Meri. I brought away three enormous volumes of press clippings, over which to warm the hands in the long twilight of a career!

But besides being transitory success it was a venture. We had not known at all how this ballet public would react to concert dancing. They let us know that we had blazed a trail.

India

Now I know as well as the reader does that Ceylon is not India. Yet my impressions of India, my feeling for it, began on that mid-December day when our ship again dropped anchor in the harbor at Ceylon. I had been dreaming for years of seeing India. *The languorous East, the mystic land*—that sort of thing. I had read all I could find on India, mainly, I must admit, on the artistic and philosophic side. I had a mind's-eye view of what I would see. White-clad, beautiful people, walking palm-shaded avenues in a state of yoga, hands joined. Heat, sun, elephants, rickshaws, women in rainbow-hued saris, men in spotless dhotis, temples, strange music, humped cattle—honored guests in the streets—walking unmolested with their human brothers and sisters.

Ceylon has great beauty. Though enervatingly hot after my winter down under, it was delightful. For me there were personal repetitions—the daily two- and three-hour rehearsals, the radio broadcasts, parties, auditions for talented dancers as well as some not so talented. The functioning of my insides developed a hitch, and it was necessary to keep my stomach so full of aspirin that I could not eat.

The debut concert was almost upon us. How the men sweated and swore to set the stage! Again there were no battens, and native stagehands seemed more trouble than help. Not only did they understand little English; they operated under a caste system that forbade an electrician to tie a rope or a stagehand to help me hang up my costumes. In the end, poor, long-suffering Mr. Longden, suspended thirty feet in the air across a bamboo pole, tied the ropes for the curtains.

With some trepidation I had decided to include *Lasyanatana*
in this first concert. That was the Indian dance I had made myself after exhaustive study of Coomaraswamy's book *The Mirror
of Gesture* and several lengthy sessions with Uday Shankar. I
was agreeably surprised. In American show business what happened with *Lasyanatana* is called "stopping the show."

There was a sort of poetic touch in the fact that we went up to
Kandy for Christmas. The big artificial lake, built long ago by the
Kandian kings . . . the necklaces of ancient palaces . . . the Temple
of the Tooth of Buddha . . . fine villas and hotels. How beautiful
it all was! And cool! On Christmas morning we opened our west-
ern-type gifts on the lawn overlooking the lake. A high hedge of
poinsettias and someone's gramophone playing "Silent Night"
reasonably satisfied our longing for a Christmas atmosphere.

At the one performance in Kandy we found to our surprise
that the audience liked best my Argentinian Gaucho dance and
my American Hopi dance.

Throughout the East I observed subsequently that audiences
did not have to "understand" a dance to like it; they just
opened their hearts, and if the dance had an emotional impact,
which, after all, is the essence of art, they accepted it with enthusiasm. A rather refreshing change, I thought, from those of
us in the West who must cavil over techniques, authenticity, and
so on, with all the head-not-heart of our book learning.

For me the highlight of the short stay in Kandy was my study
of the devil dances. I took my lessons on the hotel lawn from
Kandy's finest dancer, Ratharana, to the accompaniment of an
iron-handed drummer who, incidentally, nearly deafened me with
his complicated rhythms.

I learned three of the twenty-odd Kandian dances—the *Cobra,*
the *Elephant,* and the *Eagle.* As you would suppose, the dances,
being descriptive, are often technically very difficult, featuring
tremendous leaps. Ratharana told me that he had taught these
dances only once to a woman. She was French, he said, and I
guessed that he meant Shankar's partner, Simkie.

I learned too to put on the endlessly complicated costume
with its multiple pieces strictly dictated by legend.

Finally, with a Christmas check sent me by Lil and Dave, I bought not just a costume, but a *dream* costume. The headdress and ornaments are solid silver set with 481 semiprecious stones, among them amethysts, topazes, opals, sapphires, and aquamarines. In itself it is a rare example, the stones being of an elegance that dancers have not permitted themselves since the kings fell in Kandy. If only they had had a sister and brother-in-law to send them a Christmas check!

After dancing for a New Year's celebration at the hotel back in Colombo, getting to bed at four-thirty in the morning and having only three hours' fitful sleep, I got up to pack trunks for the ship leaving for Madras. We arrived there during the first week of January.

To my first performance at the Museum Theatre came the governor and his lady and the whole diplomatic and social set. We were assured by an authority that it was an attendance of utmost brilliance and importance. Our authority was in a position to know—he was the tax collector. It was, madam and company, he said, the biggest public ever assembled in that theater, attested to by the fact that it had been necessary to call on police to control the crush.

The following night I danced on the floodlit lawn of a British country club. The next day I went to the theater to prepare the costumes for the night's performance—a task that takes a good four hours. Whereas my first audience had been all British, my second was all Indian. I was frightened to death for my Indian dances, but these people of the languorous East reassured me by shouting with joy and by demanding an encore after each presentation.

The next morning I was scarcely out of bed when I was told that a Mr. Seshagiri was downstairs, waiting patiently for an interview. A bland, stout gentleman, he proved to be the *régisseur* of the Indian Renaissance Theatre.

It was Seshagiri who gave me an open sesame to the rich lore of the Bharata Natyam Indian dance. First, he invited me to a recital by two foremost exponents of Bharata Natyam—Varalak-shmi and Bhanumati.

These dancers were two tiny, golden goddesses, blazing in gold
and jewels and flowers. For three and a half hours they never
left the stage, and with scarcely a break they performed all the
items that comprise the traditional program. Perfectly trained in
an incredibly complicated technique, they were, to borrow from
Degas's painting days in Paris, two Indian *petites filles singes*!

At the end of the performance I was asked to make a speech,
to present garlands to the dancers and receive one myself. When
it was all over, Mr. Seshagiri undertook to make it possible for
me to study with the guru who had taught these two girls!

The very next morning I went to the little bungalow where
lived Vadivelu Pillai (the guru), the two girls, and some dozen of
their retainers and friends. It was my first understanding of the
Indian's special talent for living in unbelievable numbers in very
small spaces.

Throughout the first session the guru was skeptical. However,
he too learned something during that first lesson—namely, that I
had the capacity to work four hours at a stretch without resting
and that whereas his other pupils would burst into tears and
rush from the room, I could take any amount of correction.

Back in the hotel I lunched, rested two hours, then for three
hours practiced the steps I had learned that morning. Thus went
each of eight wonderful days.

By the third lesson old Pillai remarked that I would learn in a
month what it took his girls a year to master and that with six
months' training he'd make me the best dancer in India. At the
end of the eighth lesson he cut the time to three months. I
think the reason we got on rapidly was that I had as much admiration for him as a teacher as he had for me as a pupil. It was
stimulating to me, too, that other teachers, poets, musicians—
indeed, all the colony of dance lovers—dropped in at all my
lessons. I was, it seemed, the newest and most intriguing Bharata
Natyam phenomenon!

I have been asked how Vadivelu instructed me, for he spoke
no English and I spoke no Tamil. Although I had a young Indian translator, my guru spoke very little and never stood up
from his position on the floor. In front of his crossed knees lay

a stick like a cane, and on this he beat out the rhythm with
another stick of about eight inches. He taught by *adavus* (rhythmic combinations of movement), and someone must have demonstrated—surely, Varalakshmi, yet I have no recollection of her
slim body showing the *adavus*. Very clearly etched on my memory is Vadivelu's face—every line and every expression—and on
the periphery the sleazy rug over the hard-packed earth on
which I danced and the sound of chickens and goats in the yard
beyond. The whole experience had an aura of mysticism, and I
can only believe that something otherworldly made it possible
for me to absorb so much of the motivations and techniques of
Indian dance in so short a time.

We had to go on to Bangalore for two concerts. Between
them there came to my hotel a handsome young boy who introduced himself as Bassano Ramgopal. He spoke intelligently and
in perfect English, and I was most impressed with his knowledge
of the dance art. He was anxious to travel and have a career
and asked if I would audition him on the morrow.

From all the many auditions I had given, this youngster stood
out, impressed me most, even if he did perform a dance
of India to the music of Ravel's *Bolero*! But, I thought, perhaps
this too was a sign of seeking. He was so anxious to join us
that, after a talk with his very charming family, we agreed to
take him along.

We returned to Madras for more Bharata Natyam lessons and
to prepare for a very special performance. To my dancing lessons I had now added sessions in gesture songs with the aging
but still beautiful Srimati Gauri.

My study with the two gurus took all day. Also during this
time I was gathering invaluable knowledge from my endless dis-
cussions with the authorities of the much-beloved art.

One afternoon an old gentleman, a sufferer from elephantiasis
but an enthusiast in *talas* (rhythms), came to talk to me. Since
he spoke only Tamil, we had an interpreter. The old man grew
so excited that he would not give the interpreter time to translate and finally went so far as to tell him to sit down and
shut up!

Among other things he wanted to learn from me was whether, in Western music, we had the same *talas* that are characteristic of Eastern music and dance. I said I could not say by title, but that if he would do the various *talas,* I would see if I could match them in Spanish *taconeo* (heel work). We started off tranquilly enough, but presently his temperament began to play him false. He bagan taking it as competition and nearly destroyed himself in trying to outdo me.

The performance in Madras most unforgettable to me was the one in which Mr. Seshagiri presented Varalakshmi, Bhanumati, and me in a dance recital. Two factors served to divert some-what—if they did not wholly allay it—the rugged case of stage-fright I was working up at the very thought of facing that super-critical audience in one of their own dances.

To begin with, on the night of the recital Vadivelu, the dancers, and their considerable entourage arrived at the theater at six and proceeded forthwith to cook their supper backstage. It proved to be a real function and, I must own, rather a smelly one at that. The second distraction was the rather long ceremony of the traditional dressing of the dancers. They were comfortably ready for the performance in about three and a half hours.

The performance itself was in two parts. The first half was given over to contrasting types of western dance performed by me. The second was dedicated to Bharata Natyam items done by Varalakshmi and Bhanumati, assisted—and I think about it to this day with pride—by me. In this half I did one solo.

It is the Indian custom not to applaud at the end of a num-ber but rather at the end of a dance sequence that has particular-ly pleased. Then the guru, always present onstage, signals the performer to repeat the sequence that has been applauded.

While he was giving me lessons, Vadivelu had learned just two words of English: "awright" to convey approval, and "sit down" to order a deeper knee bend. As it turned out, he was holding a surprise in reserve.

After an applauded sequence of mine he said, "Once more." I danced the sequence three times, whether because of the audience or to give Vadivelu a chance to show off his English I cannot be sure.

It was the custom, too, for the pupils to pay the guru after a concert with gifts of garments. My mid-Victorian upbringing made this seem to me a bit improper, so I gave him a wristwatch. He was inordinately proud of it, but not for the conventional reasons, I assure you; the South Indian native is less concerned with time than any other individual on the face of the earth!

Half of Madras was down at the station to see us off after my last concert there. Dancers, poets, musicians, critics—they presented us with flower garlands and nice speeches that touched us greatly with their gentle kindness.

At Hyderabad I found myself for the first time without help in unpacking. I could always count on a good four hours for the unpacking, laying out and pressing costumes for an evening's performance. My year of intensive work had begun to catch up with me, and I had to plan also on resting in the afternoon in order to give a good performance. A further, rather startling, complication arose. I discovered that it was not possible to engage a woman to help me change during the show, that *only men were available for such work*! This struck me as a bit advanced. The upshot was that all over India I made my violently fast changes alone, difficult indeed in a climate that turns perspiration to a sort of thin body glue.

Hyderabad was ruled by a Nizam reputed to be one of the richest men in the world and one of the stingiest. The degree of wealth may have been exaggerated, but he was second to none in the degree of stinginess, if one were to believe the prevailing stories. His personal treasury was said to contain enough riches to place any European country back on the gold standard, yet people starved on unpaved streets of his capital; Golconda's famous tombs and fort were falling to ruin for lack of care, and the roads leading thither were rivers of dust.

The Nizam desired me to dance for him. Naturally, I was not to be paid. I was to consider the honor done me! Well, honor was not unknown in Texas, but it was not slavish. I did not dance in the palace. Therefore the Nizam with his court, giving a reasonable imitation of Mahomet coming to the mountain, attended my concerts in the theater.

It was in Hyderabad that I picked up the oddment of knowledge that a cobra smells like a boiled potato. With complete aplomb a dignified stagehand had warned me, "Memsahib, do not walk in bare feet or leave your trunks open. A cobra resides on our stage. As this is the mating season, regrettably he is somewhat out of sorts." I never happened to see the cobra, but I did notice a smell that I could identify only as a boiled potato. Inasmuch as it seemed unlikely that a potato was being boiled anywhere around the stage, I inquired about it. "Our cobra," I was told in the offhand way in which one might explain the conduct of an eccentric relative by "Oh, that's just Aunt Lizzie."

We went on to Poona. How beautiful the Temple of Parvati at sunset with the lovely girls, bright as the flowers they carried, trooping up the long, long stairs for their evening prayers.

Bombay . . . very cosmopolitan . . . audiences largely Parsee and generous with understanding applause. We found bonds of interest with several charming people. Leela Row, India's tennis champion, invited me to watch her lessons in Manipuri dance. Regini Devi, the Chicago dancer on whom I cast no aspersion when I say she is more Indian than the Indians, called at my hotel. We were entertained at the studio of an Indian sculptor I had met in Italy and among his guests was Nataraj Vashi, the dancer and model for several of Katchadourian's paintings. And we were able to witness a performance of Tagore's *Chitra* drama, done by graduates of his school, Santiniketan.

After Bombay, Nagpur. It afforded no hotel, so we stopped in the Dak Bungalow. Remembering my Kipling, I looked for cobras to issue from bureau drawers and for ghosts to wail under windows. But any ghosts present were outwailed by the beggars, and I was told that the cobras had moved away to avoid the mosquitoes. Sunday morning was evidently the beggar's feast day. They came from miles around to the square in front of the bungalow to get food. A motley, filthy crew—but what inexhaustible material for a painter!

Ramgopal had joined us in Bombay, and at Nagpur we went into a seven-hour workout, setting an Indian duet and Ram learning the *jarabe tapatío*. Nagpur remained a blur to us, for we left the morning after the performance.

Train travel in India in 1937 was complicated, to say the least. First of all, one had to have a bearer whose duty it was to go to the station hours ahead of train time to take possession of a compartment and hold it, the only known way of obtaining one. He had to carry with him mattresses, sheets, pillows, towels, and toilet tissue. It was the duty of Indian trains to run on wheels from here to there, not to supply the absurdities that temperamental travelers felt they must have.

At the station the bearer would take up post atop your lares and penates, having packed your luggage into the compartment and disposed the comestibles you brought along for the journey. At the last possible moment he would dash out to bring in the largest chunk of ice he could carry. Once he had made arrangements for you with the neatness of the fussiest housekeeper, the bearer took himself off to the 3rd class until your destination was reached, leaving you to your lot—i.e., endless hours of dust, heat, and stops and starts.

Calcutta: expensive, dirty, fiercely hot—but still Calcutta. The English furnished an air of mild festivity with their several clubs and evening clothes de rigueur. I had to ban parties from my agenda in favor of work and study. I assembled and rehearsed an Indian orchestra to record the dances I had learned in Madras as well as some numbers of Ram's. As always there were interviews and talks to be given at clubs and on radio. I was trying hard to see but not to be seen, except in the dance, by India. Yet inevitably there were certain duties, since I was a guest in the country, that could not be passed over.

We attended a performance given by the local dancers in Calcutta. The evening's entertainment had already started when Charles Lindbergh and his wife slipped modestly down the aisle to their seats; one could hardly say they were unobserved inasmuch as he was so tall and she so tiny. News of their presence ran around like prairie fire, and to a man the stagehands came out on the stage right in the middle of the performance, down to the footlights, leaning forward to peer at the couple with great pleasure.

We gave six concerts in Calcutta, but things did not go at all
as we had hoped. It was explained to us, surprisingly, that good
artists had come to India so seldom that the public was unable
to believe that anyone who did come was any good! I must say
that this somewhat odd view seemed more prevalent among the
British than the native public. Yet it was mainly the British
who bought the expensive seats! Ah well, we *were* covering expenses and we had known in advance that the financial going
would be tough. Moreover, I had gone to India not only to perform but also to learn. And was I learning!

Twenty-three dusty, sweltering train hours to Delhi. But
Delhi received us so warmly that our financial setback in Calcutta was forgotten.

We stayed in New Delhi. Carefully designed as a capital, it
was clean and airy with wide, long boulevards, a huge plaza, and
government buildings set in fountain-studded gardens. The first
impression was out of an exposition, one not yet opened. The
avenues were deserted; there were no cattle, no dogs, no people—
in fact, no signs of life other than an occasional speeding
automobile.

Just beyond the old city walls crouched Old Delhi, an exquisite contrast. Streets narrow as footpaths, meandering between
old buildings . . . few trees . . . air heavy with dust . . . people
everywhere. People, people, people, people, of every age, shade,
and religious belief. Looking at it all, one could only reflect
that humanity has a way of going off at some very queer tan-
gents. Gone now were the colorful saris and white dhotis of the
south. In their place we saw the forty-yard *gargari* skirt, swinging about the braceleted ankles of the women, while the men
wore jodhpurs, sack coats, and, predominantly, the fez. Behind
us were the Madras rickshaw men who, pulling two passengers,
ran with the gait and endurance of the gun dog. Here were fat,
mettlesome horses, all dressed up in feathers, beads, bells, and
floating scarves, trotting along, pulling two-wheeled tongas.

The great red mosque, the Jamma Masjid, sat lotuslike in the
midst of flights of steps leading to its sacred doors—steps not as
sightly as they should have been, for they were aswarm with

sellers of silks, used iron pots, live pigeons, odoriferous foods, and noisy sheep. It was colorful but rather paradoxical, and I found myself wishing for a much-needed Jesus to drive the money-changers from the temple.

In a sense, I am indebted to Old Delhi's *filles de joie* for my *gargari* skirt, made for me by their group tailor. We took occasion one evening to drive down what I might call the sisterhoods' street. The ladies sat on their silk-hung balconies, appearing to my somewhat myopic eyes as alluring as houris in their golden dresses and flower-decked hair. Later when I paid the tailor for my skirt, I wondered if he had stitched a bit of symbolical immorality into it so that I too might seem hourilike when I wore it.

I still have a most vivid recollection of calling for that skirt. I went by tonga, and no sooner had I arrived at the open-faced shop, which bore the sign "Paris Dressmaker," than a motley crowd gathered to stare at the spectacle of a memsahib doing business with such a man. To my relief, not to mention surprise, the skirt was ready. As I paid for it I had a sudden impulse to salute its maker with the Indian *namaste*—that greeting and farewell made by placing the palms together. At that time the salute, by tradition, was given only to Brahmins and equals; one would not thank or even notice anyone of lower caste, let alone salute him!

All this I well knew, yet I was startled out of my wits when the onlookers, seeing me make the gesture, suddenly went wild, cheering me loudly. I could hardly help feeling pleased, yet as I saw it, there was no reason for their demonstration. This man had done a good job, just as I tried to make a good job of my dancing, so why should I not salute him?

At Lahore we ran into the sort of unexpected difficulty that for us was becoming the norm of Indian theaters. We arrived in the early morning, with a concert scheduled for the same evening, but the authorities decided to hold up our material for customs duty. After hours of wrangling, the local manager, frightened by the threat of losing us altogether, finally managed to free our material, and the stage was set barely in time for the

6:30 performance. I had to go straight to the theater from customs without even washing up. I unpacked and pressed my costumes while Carreras, Averardo, and our bearer, Gana, set up. The incidental bedlam was far from soothing to my already over-wrought nerves. In India the stagehand assumes the right to at least fifteen minutes of screaming argument for every order issued. Never, never does he lose an opportunity to prove his individuality, which he finds very easy to do. For example, if he is told to pull, he simply pushes.

By the irony of fate the evening's concert was a roaring success, both artistically and financially. The management insisted on our giving two more performances and we consented, since we had a few days free and needed the extra rupees.

The added stay gave me treasured time to work for several hours a day on new dances. Also it gave me the incomparable experience of a visit to the beautiful Golden Temple at Amritsar.

This is a Sikh temple resting in the center of a lake. In the midst of the open walls under the dome sits the priest, surrounded by the flowers of the worshipers. Twenty-four hours a day, to the accompaniment of music, he reads from the holy book. In this temple any and all are welcome, and always there is food for the hungry of whatever caste or creed.

It was the temple we liked most in all of India, although there are others I shall remember too. The great reclining Buddha in the tiny open pavilion at Colombo; the simple pastoral temple outside Bangalore where Nandi, the Bull, nearly filling the tiny hall, crouches to eye you with mother-of-pearl eyes; the Snake Temple, where I worried lest I meet a live emissary of the god, and where a crone was astonished by and equally afraid of our appearance in that holy place.

I went on to Lucknow, not to perform but to study. My teacher, Ram Dutt Misra, was a delightful gentleman of some seventy years. He said deprecatingly, "My legs dance very badly now," but his face was luminous testimony to his everlasting artistry. He could make himself into anything from a Circe to a demon.

After my travail with the Spanish flamenco I did not find

Kathak too difficult, since it is based largely on rhythmic floor contacts. The East Indian, interested in cross rhythms, will go to the most extraordinary ends to learn a rhythm that an American would hear and roll off the first time he tried.

The Indians who came to watch my lessons were amazed, as the Madrasis had been, at my ability in the footwork, which to them is the most difficult part of the dance. It seemed almost as if their arms and hands could be trusted to move quite by themselves, whereas I would have to go home and struggle for hours to make mine move decently at all.

By dint of four-hour lessons every day and three-hour rehearsals after supper I managed to absorb Kathak to the point of performing it in Delhi on our return there—our last performance in India.

I think now of those months in India with a strange detachment. It seems almost that they happened to someone else. It was a time of grinding work and petty harassment. But it was also a time of great enrichment—an enrichment so profound that it has taken me nearly twenty years to savor it fully. Perhaps unwittingly I found in the golden, dusty landscape, in the great serenity of the temples, in the dark, deep eyes of simple people a clearer sense of values and a philosophy for living. I know that it was in India I reached a point at which my work became predominantly important to me, a point at which I began to feel that I was important to my work. I began to find new strengths within myself, fresh faith in my own capabilities.

To the student dancer the India of today is not the India of four decades gone. Today there are schools you may enter for study. At the time I was there you had to search out teachers and convince them first of your seriousness before they would consider any association with you. Yet the richness of great art was there then as it is now, and who were we to complain if the finding of it was difficult? Our very difficulties made it possible to gain access to the hearts and minds of the people. In every town and city there was a little group of dancers and dance enthusiasts who presented themselves at the hotel for the small courtesy of an audition, and in return those people would gladly spend days in tracking down wanted records, costume makers, and local dance festivals to see and learn from.

Artistically and practically we fought the great fight of western dancing. India had seen only Pavlova and Denishawn, who had performed solely in the major cities many years past. Opinions of western art were being drawn from the movies, which at that time ran to shoot-'em-up westerns.

At the beginning of our tour writers of our advance notices observed that of course the West must ever come to the East to learn true artistry. But by the end of the season they had seen and acknowledged the beauty, for example, of my *Madonna,* a dance of a strange religion, performed to strange music, and depicting a strange painting. I felt that on a smaller scale we did for western art what Shankar did for Indian art in the West. Great nationalists, the Indians openly loved my renderings of their own dances. The mystics declared me a reincarnation of an Apsaras, while the more practical-minded said my coming was a milestone in *Indian* art.

If I seem to exaggerate the importance of my visit to India, at least one thing is sure. Whereever we performed the theaters bought rope and electrical wiring and built proscenium arches. That, at least, was an advance!

You think the frame for a dance concert is unimportant? I still remember the pigeons of Lahore. Since the theater's construction the stage had been occupied only by a silver screen. Pigeons had made bold to nest in the flies and raise their children there, building up a thriving (not to say vocal) colony. Efforts to dispossess them for our performance proved ludicrously unavailing. Before each dance stagehands had to rush onstage with wet rags and clean up.

In the Ravel *Bolero* the curtain rises to find me prone on a Spanish shawl upstage center. With my face turned skyward, I lie there motionless for some thirty-two bars. Can you guess what I was thinking about, lying in that position on that shawl upstage center, that first night in Lahore?

I had other observers too. In my *Adoration* I raised my face and arms toward heaven in an attitude of humble prayer. There on the bridge backstage sat a half dozen Indian children watching the performance. My prayers ascended to a row of cherubim—large-eyed, dark-skinned cherubim with dangling bare feet!

The Orient

From the first we loved Rangoon. Though it was early April, the city was stifling, but so clean and lovely. If India had seemed a heroic tragedy, Burma was a lyric poem. The beautiful, shining domes of Rangoon's golden pagodas crowned a city tinctured with happiness, its people, optimists by nature, filled with laughter.

We docked in the morning and as usual we first saw to the interviews and photographers. But as soon as we could free ourselves from our appointments, we sallied forth to look for someone who would instruct me in the art of the Burmese dance. I had been told that U Po-Sein, Burma's finest dancer, was not in town, but I was determined to see for myself, or at least find out when and where I might see him.

So off we drove to the suburbs, and there up a long, dusty lane, hidden under giant banyan trees and called—of all things— Broadway, we came on the huge, meandering house that was U Po-Sein's home. Even as we arrived, U Po and his company were just climbing out of two big black Cadillacs. We put on our most beguiling smiles and went forward to plead my cause.

He was most courteous, showed us his costumes, even, to our delight, danced for us. However, he told us, through his English-speaking son, that he was an artist, *not* a teacher. So after inviting him and his family to my debut concert, which I was to give the next day, we took our leave.

The next evening U Po-Sein (decked out in pink and turquoise taffeta) and his troupe occupied one of the boxes. In another sat the governor and his party. The walls vibrated to the bravos of a capacity audience, and no one seemed to mind that I

danced miserably—or thought I had. The heat was so severe that
I felt quite faint. Yet when the concert was over, U Po-Sein
came backstage. He greeted me effusively, called me "sister,"
and commanded that I appear at his house the next morning to
learn the Burmese dance!

Early in the morning, while it was still quite cool, I presented
myself at his house. He was then sixty years old but agile as a
boy, his raven hair falling nearly to his knees. This he usually
wore done up in a knot on top of his head, but it always managed to fall down during his dance.

U Po-Sein's wife was fat, rather tall for a Burmese, and incessantly smoked the fabled "whacking white cheroot" made of
betel leaves. They had four small sons, all of them inclined to
boast of their father's great reputation and, because of it, to be
rather overbearing. The son who served as our interpreter was
doing his annual fifteen days as a Buddhist priest and so wore
the yellow robes and shaven head. There were two Misses Po-
Sein—Nellie, who was completely charming, and nine-year-old
Lily—and there was a baby aged three. The children spoke
English, but the parents did not, so all the teaching had to be
done with the son interpreting. This was particularly frustrating,
since Po-Sein was a great talker with a taste more for moralizing
about dancing than teaching it. He would not wait for his son
to translate properly, and I almost went mad trying to figure out
what this great man was really saying.

I spent four hours every morning studying. Po-Sein was
determined that I should present a Burmese dance at my second
concert, and no amount of modesty or stage fright on my part
would change his mind. Being essentially an artist and not a
teacher, he threw things at me with terrifying vigor and changed
the routine every fifteen minutes.

Following my first lesson, I spent the afternoon rushing about
town to order a costume. Costumes could be bought readymade, but, alas, not to fit elephants like me. The Burmese
dancing girl is about four feet tall, whereas I am five feet three
and a half. Moreover, Po-Sein's premier dancer was eighteen
years old and looked about ten.

I bought and brought to my second lesson the record ordered
by Po-Sein. He never put it on the machine, and with horror I
began to realize that I was going to have to make this dance myself from the steps I was managing to pick up from the maestro.
Accordingly, I went to the theater that afternoon and spent a
harrowing four hours setting the steps I had learned to the
music I had never before heard.

The next day was one of prayer, so Po-Sein could not teach. But
he assured me that he would be at the theater the following morning to fix up the dance, for, heaven help me, it had already been
announced as part of that evening's program. I spent a mad day
practicing on my own, fitting my costume, and going through a
"rehearsal" of my complicated coiffure by a local hairdresser.

Utterly exhausted, I went to tea at the home of a Dr. Ba Maw,
a charming and intellectual gentleman who spoke at length, at
my insistence, on the subject that interested me most—the Burmese dance. From this conversation we came to realize that
dear Po-Sein had been so impressed with my Spanish dancing
that he was creating a Burmese dance *à la Espagnole*—just for me!
Everyone present laughed mightily at this turn of events. My
laugh was rather sickly, however, for I had the responsibility of
doing the thing for a Burmese audience the very next night.

I twitched all night on my uneasy couch, arose at six, and
after a hasty breakfast, which was like dust and ashes in my dry
mouth, hurried to the theater. For three hours I worked arranging my costumes for the show, which was at 6:30. It began
to look as though U Po-Sein was not going to show up. Frankly, I was beginning to hope he would not, for by then I was
confused enough as it was. Finally he came, and for two hours
I skittered about the stage, almost in tears with nervousness.
Never did he do the dance twice in the same way; never did he
finish with the record; never did I find out what rhythm he kept,
if any. So much work to so little purpose! At last he went
away and I returned to the hotel for a belated lunch and a short
rest, only to start work again on that damn dance, trying to
bring order out of chaos. It was a very tired me who went
dragging into the theater at 5:30.

I got through my other thirteen dances by osmosis, thanking
God that muscles will remember when the stilled mind refuses
to function. And the closing number, the Burmese pwe? Technically, I danced it atrociously. But I have a certain talent for
characterization. I am also accustomed to saving situations, and
my costume was charming. When I walked onstage, Averardo
did not recognize me, and taking me for a Burmese lady come
to make some announcement, he waited politely, not starting
my music until I hissed at him in Italian to do so.

Public and critics were very pleased with my pwe debut. In
the end it became one of my best dances. But the time I spent
learning the pwe with U Po-Sein I could have spent learning
three items with Vadivelu!

After my third concert in Rangoon a certain Chief Thunder-
face came backstage to praise my *Umatilla Hoop Dance.* I was
so happy to see a fellow countryman in that far land! He told
us he had come to Rangoon many years before with a rodeo
company and had liked it so much that he just stayed on. He
invited us out to his place to ride some of his saddle stock.
How much I wanted to go! But by now I had learned that such
pleasures must all be sacrificed to the larger scope of learning
and to dancing.

Traveling down the Malay Peninsula, we were five: Carreras,
Averardo, Bassano, and "Jim" Rajoo, our *tabla* player and general factotum. Jim was tall, handsome, muscular, and nearly
ebony color. When he had first joined us, he had folded his
hands in the inimitable Indian way and announced, "Madam, I
am your son." I was both touched and pleased—albeit a little
startled.

From Rangoon we went to Kuala Lumpur for a concert. My
clearest memory of Kuala Lumpur is of the bathtub in the hotel.
It looked like an outsize pot for Boston baked beans. Crawling
into it with my knees higher than my ears, I sat wondering
morosely whether I would ever get out of it.

In the East they tell you that Singapore is the artist's grave-
yard. I heard that Heifetz had left the city enraged; that Galli-
Curci had canceled her second concert there; that Chaliapin had

sung to a half-empty house. I suppose I should have dreaded my performance there, but I was just too tired. After a year of steady touring one town seems from the stage very like another. The stage, with its familiar black drapes and gray floorcloth, is a world in itself. What goes on there is, somehow, outside time and space and not a part of the city around it. The illusion passes only with the fall of the final curtain. Then, tired and damp with sweat, one goes back to the dressing room to greet members of the audience, and the immediate surroundings swing back into focus.

At this "crossroads of the East" Nataraja, the god of dance, stood by us, and we played to a full house of fifteen hundred.

We sailed from Singapore for Java one morning, and the six-day sea voyage gave me a chance to loaf and refresh my spirit. I did not, of course, miss my daily practice or giving lessons in western dance to Bassano. Also I worked on the lecture I had to give in Batavia (now Jakarta). But this was idleness compared to the life I had been leading.

It took us two days to get through customs in Batavia. The red tape was a tangled skein, the urraveling a slow and pedantic business even though we had been contracted by the Kunstring itself. I commuted between the Hotel des Indes and the Customs House, and between interviews managed to get in from four to five hours' practice a day. Bassano and I were finishing off a Siva and Parvati duet, and he was still working on the *Jarabe Tapatio*. It began to seem to me that I always had six or eight half-learned dances on hand. I heartily envied those dancers who, performing in only one style, have, so to speak, only one set of muscles to school.

The Batavia theater was in the zoo, so whenever we had a moment to spare, we'd go out and watch the animals. Two baby elephants were our particular delight. One of them became so attached to Rajoo that it followed him around like an affectionate puppy.

We gave two concerts in Batavia, for the second of which Ramgopal made his debut as a Mexican dancer. He was frightened to death, but looked very handsome in his leather charro costume.

We toured Java with a car for us and a truck for the trunks and stage material. Our chauffeur was a native whose name was Moan. The spelling is purely phonetic and rhymes with *groan.* The name became thoroughly appropriate, for a more serious individual I have seldom met. He spoke very little English and everlastingly confused the two phrases "I don't know" and "I don't understand," which led to long, misunderstood dialogues between Carreras and him, which in turn reduced the rest of us to helpless laughter. Moan was also immovably stubborn and never agreed to any arrangement we had for traveling. It was only too apparent that he was accustomed to shepherding tractable tourists around his island. He just would not allow us to eat our lunch under the lovely trees. No matter how big a hurry we were in to reach the next stop and set up the show, he would detour to each and every temple, stop the car, open the door, and refuse to budge until we had descended and observed the temple. At every stop I begged him to take me to the native theater performances. He would not. I finally had to slip out of the hotel when he wasn't looking and sneak away to watch the performances, which he, doubtless, felt were not sufficiently dignified for my patronage. Blessed Moan! He never smiled once during our five weeks in Java!

We gave performances in Surabaya, Jogjakarta, Solo, Malang and Semarang and returned for two more shows in Batavia. I gave several conferences on Indian dance on this tour with Ramgopal and myself as demonstrators.

The area through which we drove was always lushly green, starred with orchids and so continuously beautiful that one sometimes had to raise one's eyes to a stark volcano to rest from the surrounding riot of greenery. They say that God walked the roads to Java and brought them beauty. Certainly, being Javanese, the gods *walked,* for every road was filled with laughing brown people in bright garments. Indeed, there was never a moment in the city when the car was not passing workers in groups, beggars, priests, rich men and poor. There were times when it was pretty unnerving, for there were no comfort stations and few bushes such as one may sneak behind in countries

less fair. But, we kept telling ourselves, we could not allow
minor inconveniences to obtrude on our appreciation of such a
fairyland!

The culture superimposed on the Javanese was characteristic
of the Dutch—a slow pedantry of thought, good humor and delight in good living, cleanliness, and interest in things cultural.
Racial barriers seemed nonexistent, and the children of mixed
marriages were well-made, vigorous, and very handsome.

Jogja and Solo interested me most among the cities, for in
them flourished the classical dance of Java. These two schools
were supported by the princes of the respective cities, and some
of the principal dancers came from the royal family. I had an
excellent opportunity to study the teaching methods, for both
princes invited us to attend classes in the three-year course at
the palace. We watched lessons for beginners, second-year, and
third-year dancers. Classes were held from 7 to 11 P.M. every
evening. I came to wonder when the Javanese ate. As a matter
of fact, the climate imposed a special routine of living on the
inhabitants. They arose at five or six in the morning and went
about their business until about one. From two to four in the
afternoon everyone returned home and went to bed. There was
a law (and it was enforced) prohibiting any noise during those
hours, and even the tooting of a motor horn was a violation. At
four everyone came back to life, and "day" went on until
around midnight.

In spite of Moan we saw as many popular performances of the
dance-drama as we could. We watched the royal Sriwedari performance in Solo, and we went to the tent-housed shows of the
average folk. Night after night they performed the same Rama-
epic dramas that had been enacted for centuries, always to a full
house. I shall never forget the enchantment of those shows—the
heady, hypnotic music; the stately, stylized movements of the
actors; and the strangely exciting smell of the native cigarettes,
smoked in the audience and spreading like an incense over the
whole.

Along the endless string of unpacking, mending, rehearsing,
dancing, repacking, traveling, da capo, were the bright beads of

my trips to the Javanese theaters and costumers and, best of all, my lessons, which I took whenever and wherever time permitted. During our more extended stay in Batavia I took daily three-hour lessons with Soerharsono, former soloist of the Jogja school and presently a medical student. His sister was a serimpi dancer whom I had met and found to be thoroughly charming. I took my lessons on the open balcony of my hotel room, over-looking the inner park, where regal peacocks spread their tails and uttered their incredible cries under orchid-draped trees.

Surabaya was the most modern of the towns, outside of the capital, and Malang the most "native." In the latter our hotel stood on a bluff overlooking the river. Cool and beautiful, this river was a spectacle in itself, for the whole village came down to its banks for all the necessities of living. At fifty yards' distance from each other bathed brown young men and beautiful-bodied girls. Fat babies paddled in the shallows. Small boys swam in the pools. Women washed bright batiks along the banks, and in between, upstream and down, folk washed their teeth, hair, dogs and cattle, and, in this same lively little river, performed certain other functions I won't mention. And always there were song and laughter everywhere. Thus might have been the Garden of Eden—if it hadn't been for that mischievous snake.

In such an environment who can blame the young manager of the hotel for his heady flights of fancy? He told me in no un-certain terms that he was a dancer of outstanding quality; as a matter of fact, he said, he had given up dancing because he had found it too easy to be interesting. The first time he had heard Granados's music he had improvised a perfect Spanish dance. He assured me that the first time he had tried he had risen on his toes and performed an entire Rachmaninoff prelude; that every teacher he had ever been to had told him, after the first lesson, that they could teach him nothing, for he knew all. How I envied him! Not his "abilities," which, happily, I did not ob-serve, but his happiness and belief in the hypnotic power of his own words. I would stay in the Eden of Malang forever, could I but attain this Brahmananda of self-confidence!

A return engagement in Singapore—one performance at the big

English theater and two at the "vernacular" theater. Then we set sail on the S.S. *Conte Rosso.* Life, especially in the theater, is like bacon—a streak of fat and a streak of lean. Our streak of fat had been very wide. Manila was certainly our streak of lean!

I hadn't been in my own country for five years, and as we sailed toward the Philippines I thought, "At least here I won't be a foreigner!" The boat docked at 5:30 P.M. June 17. With all our papers in order we took our places confidently in line, moving toward the official table. They would not let us land! Well, they could scarcely stop me, as I was an American. But our two Italians and the two Indians—that was something else.

Certainly I was not going to get off alone, so we stood miserably on the deck, watching our sixty-odd trunks and crates being lowered to the wharf. Three hours and forty dollars of palm oil later we descended, just as the *Conte Rosso* was about to leave the berth. But our troubles had just begun. Authorities insisted the Indians had to go into detention. More money changed hands, and Ram and Jim made their grateful escape into the town. Then the authorities would not release our material without a two-thousand-dollar bond! It was already night; the customs office closed down; we had had no supper, so we left our precious luggage and went into town. The local manager who had drawn up the contract with Longden did not appear during all this bewildering time. So the next morning— the very day of our scheduled opening concert—Carreras sallied forth to look up this personage and solve the bond difficulty. Jim went down to the dock to watch over our luggage. Averardo went to the Italian consulate. Bassano went to the British consulate. And I stayed in my hotel room next to the phone, as a clearing house of news to the far-scattered company. No one knew what would happen next. Would we get in and give the concert? Or would we leave on the next boat—whenever the next boat might be.

To add to our consternation we found that our appearance had not been announced at all! Perhaps this local lesion of contract was just as well, for it was three days later before we saw our goods arriving at the theater.

And now we were faced with the sad fact that we had no alternative to giving concerts in Manila. We had to, for we hadn't enough money left to catch the next boat out! The money that had been flowing out of our pockets in such a steady stream was the money we had been saving for the long jump to the States! So there was really nothing left to be decided, except to try to salvage the situation with hard work.

Carreras ran around like mad, getting out enough publicity to appraise the public of our postponed concert. At least I could not complain about interviews taking up all my time, and I spent my days in hours of hard practice and in taking lessons in Philippine dances with Mme. Reyes-Tolentino.

Of our four contracted concerts we gave only two, taking our hard-earned box-office assets then and rushing away from this puzzling place, the same where the immortal Argentina had played to a house of twenty-odd patrons! Some balm was applied to my wounds by the Spanish colony, for wherever I did my Spanish dances for Spaniards, heartening "olés" rang out, and I was enthusiastically bracketed with La Argentina and La Argentinita.

Have you heard the old song:

> "We'll all go down in China
> On a lousy Dollar liner . . ."

Believe me, nothing ever looked so magnificently *un*lousy to me as the Dollar liner *President McKinley* when we stepped aboard her on June 30, bound for China.

July in Hong Kong—and such heat as makes dying of it seem quite possible! In every other way our stay in the city was just about perfect. For one thing, we spent five days in Hong Kong and gave three concerts; I always enjoy places where I can work with satisfaction. Too, the local manager had done a superb job of advance publicity and was, himself, an extremely charming gentleman. Last, but surely not least, we had full houses and headline reviews.

As indicating China, Hong Kong was, of course, pretty diluted. Nevertheless, we saw all we could of the local theater. We thought we would be seeing the real China later, for Mr. Longden

had booked a tour of the principal cities immediately following
our tour of Japan.

Alas, this was not to be. I may have been the last western
artist to play the fine, air-conditioned theater in Hong Kong for
a very long time; shortly after we left, bombs dropped on the
city.

We saw more of Shanghai in our one-day stopover than we
did of Hong Kong in five days; that is what work does for one.
In Shanghai we behaved just like average tourists, browsing
through the native quarter, the Mandarin's Garden, the Willow
Pattern Teahouse.

Back on board, the heat was so intense that sleeping in our
staterooms was out of the question and we spent the night on
deck, wide-eyed and sweltering. On the morning of departure
we watched from the deck the dockside entertainers. A clever
woman sleight-of-hand artist and her tumbling children were
quite good enough for the Keith circuit. A comic wrestler whose
specialty was wrestling himself was authentically funny. Yet we
were well satisfied to cast off and head for open sea with its
welcome breezes. I got back to my schedule of three-hour
practice with intermittent plunges in the ship's pool.

I am not one of those people who have hunches that pay off,
so nothing told me that I was about to fall in love with the land
lying just ahead of our cleaving prow. Indeed, I spent a good
deal of time fretting about Japan's customs routine. I could
have saved myself the trouble. We had a foretaste when the ship
docked at Kobe. We went ashore and everything was delightful.
Everyone was so kind and polite. Everything was so sweet and
clean. There was beauty of line and color everywhere, from
"Theater Street" to the distant cone of Fujiyama.

Docking at Yokohama on the fifteenth, we found the customs
officers courteous, considerate, and efficient, always an excellent
introduction to any country, especially for those poor beasts of
burden among us who travel about with a "shell" of 67 trunks
on our backs.

We were to be in Japan some three months and decided to
rent a house in Tokyo. Of course we couldn't exactly afford to

lay off, but with our China tour canceled and a vacation of a
kind thrust on us, we were determined to enjoy it.

Commuting from Yokohama, we took several days to locate a
house suitable to rent, for while the Japanese house is startlingly
clean and practical for those accustomed to the mode of living,
we doubted that our western-trained selves would take to eating,
sleeping, writing, and living generally on matting floors. At last
we had the good fortune to discover the home of a British
family that was spending the summer by the sea. The house,
situated in a park studded with a lake and beautiful trees and
flowers, was amply large for our party. We engaged a Japanese
cook and amah, making it possible to move in within four days
of our arrival at Yokohama, a hot meal awaiting us.

We had overtaken Mr. Longden at last, and our party at the
Azabu-ku "home" numbered six plus the house servants. There
was a lot of work to do. All the trunks had to be unpacked and
the material reconditioned. My costumes had taken an awful
beating and cried piteously for cleaning and mending. Many of
them, I found, had given up the ghost completely. We engaged
two seamstresses to come in by the day; during the winter they
worked for the Kabuki Theatre.

They made exquisite new editions of several costumes—Spanish, classical and modern, besides several Japanese costumes I
needed as I began learning new dances. The seamstresses were
a gay and cheery pair. They picked up English quite rapidly,
and Averardo, who spent most of his time happily in the service
wing, kept them in a continual state of giggles.

Of course it was not all work. We explored the beautiful city
and its environs, shopped, enchanted, along the Ginza, often
attended the Kabuki and Takarazuka theaters, and watched the
festivals of fireworks over the river. We were even so fortunate
as to be invited to a performance of Noh drama.

As always I found audiences in theaters and people in the
streets as clear and exciting a lesson in ethnic movement as any
learned from the theater performances. On the stages were the
technique and tradition; in the streets was the universal underlying motivation.

It is no trite saying that "one must walk before one can dance." So I studied the lovely walk of the ladies of Japan. Though Japanese businessmen were more than likely to be wearing western suits, not a western female dress was to be found in all Tokyo.

My greatest delight was a neighborhood shopping street near the house. Here we would walk on cool evenings—I should say, evenings less hot. There were no tourists, no foreigners but ourselves. We could converse only in sign language, but this merely lent enchantment to the adventure in a country where everyone is unfailingly polite and good-humored.

In the shops a riot of silks of incredible variety of design hung temptingly from walls and ceilings. Silk and paper flowers bloomed in slender vases, looking real enough to be artificial. Each shop, raised some three feet above street level, was open-faced and bright with paper lanterns. There were shops that carried only getas—maiko getas of lacquered wood, six inches high and embossed with golden storks; cork-soled getas, straw getas, silk getas, getas in every color, material and size, except big enough for clumsy western feet! Another shop whirled with paper parasols and umbrellas of every possible size and design. A shop next door sold *furoshikis,* those silken squares of bright and beautiful design in which every self-respecting Japanese wrapped bundles for carrying; paper-wrapped bundles were considered vulgar. One shop *gave* me a *furoshiki* rather than let me disgrace myself by walking out with a paper-wrapped purchase.

One shop sold only the pads, cords, and scarves in bright colors with which the Japanese woman dons her complicated obi. Another sold decorative scrolls; another, china teapots; still another, marriage wigs, for brides must wear a certain hair-dress, and because the modern girls were beginning to bob their hair, they would buy a wig for the nuptials (the broad white band around the forehead being to hide the legendary horns!). All the way along, in front of the established shops, peddlers of new and second-hand wares spread out their mats to display a tempting mélange of objects. How I wished we were rich in empty trunks!

Wandering one evening through this section, we stopped to
watch a play performed on the pavilion stage before a temple.
It was a continuous performance, attended by any and all who
cared to stand and watch. The players were all men, the tale
they enacted an old legend, the costumes brilliant and effective.
A lone foreigner, standing among the gentle Japanese, I loved
this performance even more than those of the formal theaters,
for here was art "of the people, by the people, for the people."

The very first day in our new house we moved all the furniture out of the dining room and converted it into a studio.
There I spent the better part of every day. In the morning I
gave Bassano a three-hour lesson in western dance format. In
the afternoon I did three hours of my own work.

Meantime, the living room was converted into an office where
Mr. Carreras, Mr. Longden, and Mr. Okiyama worked all day.
The garage was dedicated to Averardo and his work on the stage
material. Jimmy drummed or alternately rushed about the city
on errands. Already he had picked up a working knowledge of
the Japanese language. In spite of the enervating heat we were a
busy household.

When evening finally brought a ghost of cool air, it was our
great delight to bathe and dress in Japanese kimonos and loll on
the terrace while we went over the day's problems. Problems
there were in plenty, for war clouds were gathering, which might
make the tour of Japan and China impossible. And the Latin
American tour that was to follow was some months away.

I started my lessons in Japanese dancing. The Kokusai Bunka
Shinkokai (Society for International Cultural Relations) recom-
mended as teacher the wife of an authoritative writer on Japanese dance and herself a dancer and teacher of repute. She spoke
no English, so her husband came along to my lessons to translate.

The first evening Mme. Kodera showed me several classical
and folk dances. As usual it was taken for granted that I would
not be able to absorb any of them much under two years. I
convinced them that I was anxious at least to try, and it was arranged that they would come to the house three evenings a week
and give me private lessons. After a few lessons the Koderas

In a prologue in San Antonio, 1922.

La Vida Breve (Manuel de Falla), Paris, 1930.

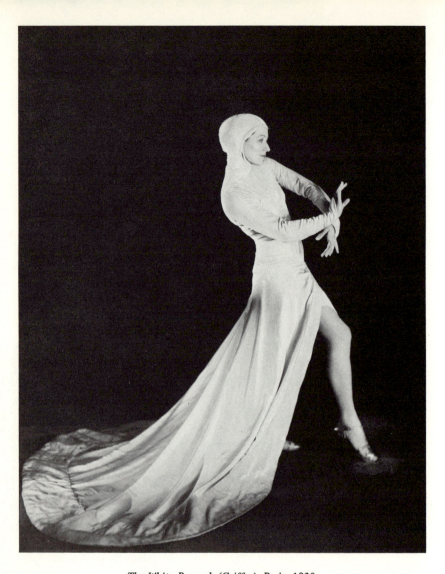

The White Peacock (Griffes), Paris, 1930.

Salacot with Ram Gopal (Choreography, Tolentino), Manila, 1937.

Debut in *Bharata Natyam* (Choreography, Vadivelu Pillai), Madras, 1937.

Echigo-Jishi, Tokyo, 1937.

were very impressed with my speed in learning. The teaching
system was for the teacher to do the dance over and over again
until the pupil grasped it by osmosis. As Mme. Kodera repeated
the dance several times I would write down the number and
form of the steps. I drew on the terminology of Hindu, Spanish, and ballet dancing. Anyone who had chanced to look over
my notes would have been able to take them only for psychotic
images of a mental patient. However, checking and properly
correcting them, I would spend several hours between lessons in
fitting the music and steps together, and the hardest work was
done. The next lesson would be spent on the gestures and the
next on polishing the whole. Thus I learned six Japanese classical dances in five weeks. The Koderas became convinced that
my speedy grasp of technique was largely due to my counting
the music, and so to help me Mme. Kodera learned the numerals
in English and called them out as she danced. It was sweet of
her but, in a seriocomic way, distressful for me, because she invariably skipped seven and twelve, and when she came to the
teens, would take two beats for each number—for example, "sir-
teen, fo-teen, if-teen." It grew quite confusing.

One day the Koderas took me around to all the shops that
sold theatrical supplies. The making of stage props had always
fascinated me. The prop makers allowed us to go up to the
second floor, where neatly displayed samples of the hundreds of
props used in the Japanese theater were explained to me. Here
I ordered my Echigo *jishi* "hat," my masks, my chrysanthemum
circles, my cherry blossoms, all while we sat on the matting
floor and sipped tea. We went on to a tiny house, spotlessly
clean with its sliding paper doors, matting floor, a single vase of
beautifully arranged flowers, where I selected fans—and sipped
more tea. Then to the wigmakers to order three wigs, and sip
more tea. This shop, open all along the front, was on the street
floor. Imagine the giggling joy of Japanese urchins as they
watched the blue-eyed western lady trying on Japanese gentlemen's wigs! We went to another shop to order *tabi*, white for
feminine dances, black for Echigo *jishi*. It was all such fun!

For kimonos Mr. Okiyama took me to a street where secondhand geisha garments were sold. The truly elegant geisha wouldn't be caught dead wearing the same kimono twice. So I bought these sumptuously beautiful silken robes for a song. Of course, each costume must be carefully matched to obi, tie, and cord, and the obis mounted in the way Japanese performers mount them for speed in donning, for in the normal way, with the clever assistance of an expert's hand, the obi takes a good half hour to put on.

We felt several earthquakes while we were in Tokyo. During the worst one we all jumped from our beds and ran down to spend the night in the garden. I recalled the many pitiful stories Mr. Okiyama had told me about the truly bad quakes of the past. The Japanese will explain that the quake that shakes sideways is not dangerous, but the one that shakes up and down is. (I did not develop enough calmness of nerve to analyze the direction of the shaking.) In the yearbook we found a statement illustrative of the great Nipponese nationalistic spirit. "Japan and Italy have more earthquake shocks than any other countries on earth, but Japan beats Italy."

During this period of intensive study—not only was I learning Japanese dancing, I was trying to sort out and assimilate the extraordinary mass of dance knowledge I had so recently and hectically acquired in other areas of the Orient—I had the misfortune to develop a bad charley horse. The doctor put me in a splint, and for five days I had to content myself with my daily lessons to Bassano and "chair practice," as I termed dancing my eastern repertoire with only my arms. It probably did me a lot of good, but it was most irksome. Trips to the dentist during this interval did not make me any easier to get along with.

On an oppressively hot day in mid-August seven Leica experts came to the house. Averardo hung black drapes across the back of the terrace, and I changed from costume to costume while those enthusiastic Japanese—instinctively magnificent photographers—burned up over 400 films on me. As hot as the work was, it proved worthwhile, for out of the lot we got some extraordinarily fine shots, and the Leica people made up 3,000 copies of a fine poster, which they presented to us.

About this time the Kokusai Bunka Shinkokai asked me to give an illustrated lecture on the Indian origins of Japanese dance. This was certainly a large order, but Carreras accepted the invitation and I in turn accepted it without question. I had a fortnight in which to pull the material together. I plunged into a welter of reference books. I wrote far into the night, for of course I could not give up my dancing lessons and daily practice of my repertoire, which now numbered over a hundred dances. There was to be a display of my ethnic costumes in connection with the lecture, so I selected about fifty of the best and many instruments and accompanying jewelry and props. The costumes were displayed on mannequins. Where but in Tokyo would one find small Japanese mannequins for the Oriental costumes and tall blond mannequins for the western costumes? We worked six hours the day before the lecture, arranging the display with identifying cards. It all looked beautiful, and like a fond mama I just loved it!

The lecture went off very well. I spoke in English, but at the end of each paragraph a young Japanese woman interpreted. This made the whole business incredibly long, but the Japanese seem accustomed to long affairs, and nobody was bothered by it but American me. The lecture was illustrated by movements and dances, Bassano doing some of the East Indian ones, while I did others plus the debut of my first Japanese dance. The K.B.S. took movies of the dances, and the Museum of the Theatre took the manuscript for their reference files.

It became increasingly apparent that we would have to leave this lovely country immediately after my five Hibya Hall concerts, for Tokyo was boiling with military preparations and sinister with practice blackouts. All day every day the streets were crowded with truckloads of friends and relatives going to the station to say good-bye to departing soldiers. It is the custom when a man is called to the colors for all his friends to give him farewell parties. These are very serious affairs, as it is expected that he will either come back a hero or honorably get himself killed. The parties were elegant, in keeping with the status of the "hero." In one case we knew of a very wealthy gentleman, feted

for two weeks, departed in a cloud of glory, only to be rejected
at training camp for some such silly thing as flat feet! Poor
man! Being too mortified to return home, he went abroad on a
long, long trip.

On all the downtown streets dainty girls stood with broad
pieces of white linen in their hands. These were belts and were
to be covered with thousands of French knots in red string, each
knot embroidered by a different person so that the thousands of
knots might keep the soldier wearer of the belt from harm. The
girls stood all day on the street, getting their belts made for
husband or brother or sweetheart. We ourselves sewed many
knots, but as the string had to be bitten off, we finally stopped
out of concern for our teeth.

When the war finally closed in and our Japanese tour had to
be canceled, along with the one in China, the scheduled opening
at the Bellas Artes in Mexico City was still far off and there
were the five people in our company to feed, house, and, God
willing, pay. The jump to America would be long and expensive, and the prospect of making any money soon looked dim.
Sad decisions had to be made and carried through. We decided
to go on to California and, from there, try to advance the dates
of our concerts in Mexico.

Mr. Longden, armed with photographs and press notices,
sailed for the States. It grieved us that we had to arrange to
send our beloved Rajoo back to India immediately upon our
departure. We booked passage for Bassano to go with him, but
he had made many friends in Tokyo and was determined to wait
there until he could finance going on to America to continue
his career.

I am writing now from a little diary I used to keep, although
"diary" is too formal a word for the little daybook in which I
kept notes for my weekly letters to Lil. Here are some excerpts
from the days leading to our departure from Japan: "Tears and
hysterics. Also managed to work on the records (sorting, label-
ing, and packing for shipment). Ran through the next two programs. Danced the 30 dances I must still do in Tokyo. Packed
after supper. Bed early." (I should hope so!)

This was the day after my debut in Tokyo. There follow several blank pages; what with packing and dancing I had no time to make notes. Only the day of departure was written in. I planned to do more after boarding the boat.

We arose very early indeed to finish the last-minute packing, for the trunks were to leave for Yokohama by truck at nine-thirty. Then I had to check over the house to be sure all the linen and silver were there and that the teapot we had broken had been replaced.

With our 13 suitcases we were all ready to leave when who should drive up but Mr. Takano. In his arms he carried a great square package. This he gave me with grave courtesy and gratitude as a gift from the K.B.S. It was so generous and I was so grateful—but another great package to add to our 67 trunks? Oh no!

Fast upon Mr. Takano's heels came all our neighbors, many of whom we had never seen before, wanting to bid us good-bye. And on the dock in Yokohama we were met by the cook, the amah, and the two little seamstresses, who gave us armloads of flowers.

The *Chichibu Maru* pulled away from the pier on that afternoon of September 24, breaking the varicolored paper streamers that bound our hands to those of friends on land. Rajoo was there, tears streaming down his face as he waved a bright *tenugui*. On deck we three, Carreras, Averardo, and I, found our own eyes wet. We loved Rajoo and we loved Japan so much.

I had been gone from Japan many years before I learned that popular gossip had marked me as a spy! If they actually believed such a thing, it could never have been suspected from their kindness and courtesy, which remained unfailing. For my own part, I loved them all dearly. Even the gossip was to be regarded in a glamorous light. How many of us can, even innocently, find ourselves regarded as a Mata Hari?

Hawaii, the States, and Mexico

I am always a bad sailor if the sea moves at all, particularly if I am tired out. So I spent a couple of days in my berth, dreaming of "green fields and pastures new—anything that would stay still under my feet! Yet the *Chichibu Maru* was a wonderful liner. On the top deck was a small Japanese house that, since the *Chichibu* was queen of the line, was the "royal" suite. The captain courteously offered me this for my daily practice. Quiet, isolated, the walls of translucent *shojis* opened to reveal rooms carpeted in padded matting, each room empty of all save a single wall scroll with a flower arrangement beneath. It was an impressive atmosphere in which to work on my many new eastern dances.

In crossing the 180th meridian we acquired two September twenty-ninths, but I was sick for one of them, so the novelty did me no good. Yet in spite of the unpacific Pacific it was one of the happiest crossings I have ever made. There were wonderful parties nearly every day—parties so unique and beguiling that even the most blasé of the passengers wholeheartedly entered into the fun. One evening we watched fireworks bloom kaleidoscopically against the night sky, spangling the rolling waves with myriad reflections. One long, sunny afternoon, given paints and pottery pieces, we all became artists in ceramics and saw our creations baked in electric ovens on deck. One dinner hour the entire first-class deck was transformed into a Japanese garden. Wisteria climbed up carved lattice panels to interspersed bright lanterns. We sat on colorful silken cushions around low lacquer tables. Each course was served in ceremonial fashion by our regular waiters, who turned up garbed as geishas. Although they

129

performed the ceremonial service with efficiency and grace, we could not help laughing at the sight of their familiar masculine faces beneath wondrously complicated feminine wigs and heavy makeup. Humorous too was the getup of some of the passengers; we had been requested to wear kimonos to dinner, and most had complied to the extent of whatever they happened to have bought in Japan or could borrow from fellow passengers. Happily, I had a real obi to wear with my kimono, so I had an edge on my countrymen, and when I entered, I received a pleasant round of applause from the Japanese.

Accustomed to entering the States via New York, I dreaded all American customs formality. But on the day we arrived at Honolulu our inspector was suffering from a particularly bad hangover, and he also wanted to get away to the ball game, so he put us through in jig time.

Our local manager met us on the dock with beautiful gingerflower leis of greeting. She proved to be not only an efficient and sympathetic manager but a charming and hospitable hostess.

Through her I got in touch with a teacher of the hula as soon as I arrived and arranged to take lessons every day of our stay. Until then my sole hula instructor had been Lilian, who had gone to Hawaii with David when he was stationed there in 1924. At that time she had had the rare privilege of working with the great Ana Hila, last representative of the old classic style of technique. I have always liked the classic style better than the modern, but my repertoire was limited, and I was bent on enlarging it.

We gave two concerts in Honolulu, one in the concert hall and the other at the College of Fine Arts, where I danced in the patio of the beautiful Spanish-style building. The informality of my surroundings gave me a happy feeling of oneness with my audience.

The "dividend" of my first concert was a fortuitous one, for it was after this performance that I met Juanita, native author of the best seller *The Wonderful World I Live In*. This book, written with enthusiasm and love of her fellow man, she

had done after her return from an around-the-world trip that
she had made armed only with her optimistic courage and her
willingness to work her way wherever she was. She had managed to visit all countries of the Orient, and because her skin
was dark and her heart honest, she had been made welcome in
homes and temples generally closed to the white-skinned sophis-
ticate. Half Hawaiian, "half soldier," she was the possessor of a
rare wisdom and the capacity for living fully every hour.

Juanita and I became great friends. Out on Waikiki Beach
with only her mongrel puppy for an audience, she taught me the
fine ancient hulas of her people—just because she liked me! I
would not have insulted her by mentioning money; I had learned
not to from the Maoris!

One enchanted evening we saw Winona Love dance. Since
her childhood she had been acclaimed Hawaii's greatest *olapa*,
yet when barely twenty she had married and "retired." On the
occasion when we saw her she had been persuaded to make a
special appearance to honor some visiting political celebrities.

Against the sensuous background of the tropical garden, attired in a black satin holoku and garlanded with dozens of
fragrant white leis, Miss Love was a living idyllic poem. With
scarcely any movement of feet or hips, her flowing hands flow-
ered on the white vines of her arms while her lovely face, as en-
raptured as that of a dreaming child, lifted to express all the
naive joy of a tropical civilization now lost in the mists of long-
gone yesterdays.

With infinite regret we sailed from Hawaii early in October.
We were loaded up to our ears with leis, and the beautiful voices
of a mixed double quartet sang "Aloha Oe" as the ship pulled
away. Passing Diamond Head, Carreras, Averardo, and I threw
our fragrant garlands into the sea, for it is always said that this
is the secret charm that brings the traveler back to the islands;
and who would not wish to return? I vowed that I, for one,
would look upon those shores again and on the mystic East that
lay beyond them as well. I never have. There have been wars.
There has been a new life to build. There have been many obstacles. Perhaps it was a kindly karma; perhaps wars and

continuing unrest have changed the lovely, exotic lands too
much. Perhaps I am happier, remembering the East as I first
saw it.

When we arrived in Los Angeles, Lilian and Longden were
there to meet us, Lilian looking perfectly beautiful and Longden
running up and down in a nervous swivet, afraid we had missed
the boat.

After a few happy days of reunion Longden hurried off to
Mexico City to see if the personal approach would help where
letters had failed—to wit, advancing our dates in that city. Vain
hope! Who ever heard of a Mexican hurrying things up? After
a month of telegram-punctuated waiting in California we decided
to give up and go on to New York to spend Christmas there
with Lil and Dave.

We routed through San Antonio, wiring Longden to come
up from Mexico to meet us between trains and tell us what was
happening. Poor Longden got as far as the border, where he
allowed himself to tell the Mexican officials in that English
fashion of his that they were inefficient; for this information
they put him in jail. We did not see him in San Antonio, therefore, but we wired the money to bail him out. It was hardly
surprising that he did not like Mexico or Mexican ways. The
climate and food did not agree with him. He did not understand—hence did not like—the people, and what in his profession
was worse, the people did not like him. I think he longed for
Melbourne—and Paris—from the moment he landed in Los
Angeles, for American business methods drove him crazy.

Apparently his unfortunate Mexican experience did for him,
for after a short visit in New York he bade us farewell and left
for Europe. It saddened us to see him go, for he had a truly
magic touch in theater management and was, besides, a very fine
human being.

Soon after we arrived in New York, Carreras found a large
studio in the fifties. There we put all the trunks and installed the
typewriter and gramophone—the instruments of our labors. Every
day we went there to work—Averardo to refurbish the stage
materials, Carreras to write endless business letters, I to dance.

Early in December Carreras closed a contract with Columbia Concerts. A few days later I danced six consecutive hours for Mr. Coppicus, who wished to select numbers for the concert he had set for December 12. After some deliberation Mr. Coppicus decided on an all-ethnic program. He said it would be something new in the city. I had some reservations but deferred to his judgment.

He was proven eminently right, for the concert was a fine success. I danced two and a half hours and they demanded still more—this from a New York audience that was generally halfway to Brooklyn by the last curtain! Thus reassured, Mr. Coppicus announced two more concerts for January as publicity preparation for the tour we would make in 1939 under his management.

By now it was Christmas.

Lilian, Dave, and I had not been together on this day of days since 1931. We made a crechè and bought a tree, a great turkey dinner, and one hundred eighty gifts to open among us. We had everything and we had each other. How one remembers one's Christmases! The happiest one, the gayest one, the merriest one, the most exciting one; all but the first and last one.

In the evening we went to a neighborhood theater to see *The Wizard of Oz*, something I had loved since I was three. Then the four of us skipped all the way home, singing "The Wonderful Wizard of Oz" at the top of our lungs. We were followed for a good half block at one point by a highly suspicious policeman.

The days sped by, filled with work and happiness—a most excellent combination. Then it was January 30 and I gave my two concerts—a matinee and an evening show. That day in two very different programs I danced some thirty-odd numbers. When it was over, I was tired, but a *good* tired.

With a flurry of packing and last-minute shopping we at last were on our way to San Antonio, where we were to stop over on our way to Mexico. Longden had set up a concert date in my old home town. We were met at the train by a girl we had long ago "adopted" as a member of the Hughes family. Olivia promptly elected herself my social secretary and backstage helper.

It had been some ten years since last I had danced in San Antonio, the city that had been the scene of my first feeble terpsichorean efforts. Now I had returned, having woven a girdle of experience of ten years of round-the-world travel and study, with the result that once I was in the theater for the performance, my "home" city became every city. It could have been Kuala Lumpur or Geelong or Gualeguaychú—just another town to weave into my girdle. As always I wanted my audience to like me, but they too were shadowy, faceless. Consequently, when, after my first group of dances, I realized just where I was, it came with something of a shock. I thought, "Here I am in front of my drapes, on my own floorcloth. I am doing the same dances, making the same bows that I have made before Britons and Hindus and Japanese and Viennese and goodness knows how many other peoples. But these people out there tonight are the boys and girls I was raised with and *their* boys and girls whom I have never seen. Still this *is* only another concert in a long succession of concerts, another town in a long itinerary of towns. And this approval, this applause, means no more, no less, than the approval and the applause of any other audience."

Nevertheless, the post-concert reception took on a very different character from the hundreds of other receptions. Instead of signing programs and murmuring, "Thank you so much!" in several different languages to shoals of perfect strangers, I felt myself swept up in a crowd of old friends, calling out half-forgotten nicknames, remembering hoary local jokes. There was a schoolteacher who had always regarded me with a wan patience whose face was now wreathed in smiles. There were mothers with their children, smiling at me tentatively, not quite sure of themselves. There was a boy I used to dance with, grown stout and pompous with success; a girl I went to college with, presenting a daughter taller than herself. And there was my beautiful singing teacher, happily trailed by an adoring rich husband. So many familiar faces! They had grown a little fatter or a little thinner and grayer. Was it possible? And in so short a time? When it was all over, I looked in my mirror. Why, of course. I too had grown a little thinner, and in my hair small

white wings had begun to show. I could not believe it! Why, I
had been dancing only . . . Good heavens! Not *that* long! Not
fifteen years!

Just after mid-February we left San Antonio for Old Mexico. Olivia, on sabbatical leave from her teaching, went with us,
for I could not bear to leave all friendships behind me. I was
going to the land where I had made my first foreign appearance
twelve years earlier. I remembered the flowers of Xochimilco,
the charros in the park on Sunday mornings, the courtesy and
appreciation, the culture and dignity of Mexico. And now I had
completed my first round-the-world tour and was commencing
my second. Once more it all seemed very exciting, full of
potentialities!

I yield to no one in my affection and admiration for Mexico. I was so happy to be going back to dance in a country
where the rewards of my first appearance, more than ten years
earlier, had been so much better than I deserved. Now I would
be able to prove that I had grown as a creative artist. As it
turned out, I had to learn all over again that Mexico has ways of
doing things that are very much her own.

Supposing in my innocence that I had some right to be, I
was very proud of my costumes for this engagement, all sixty-
seven trunks of them, exquisitely packed. We got them through
the American customs rather easily. But at the Mexican customs
on the other side, oh my! We opened every last one of the
trunks and spent our entire first afternoon across the border
arguing, on an icy station platform, with officials of the Mexican
customs. Word had spread around that a couple of "rich
artists" were going through. Officials collected like buzzards on
a carcass. Shortly we divined what was needed—palm oil! It is
one thing to know it is indicated, quite another to know how
and precisely when to apply it. We soon discovered a bad flaw
in the proceedings. The official who looked to be in charge of
examining our trunks was not, it seemed, the right official for
this particular job, and it would be necessary to start all over
again. We began to feel both sorry for ourselves and indignant,
a chemistry of emotion I do not recommend. So far as we

could discern, the only really nice people anywhere in the vicinity were the peons who diligently moved the heavy trunks. Although the official had with great carelessness flung their contents around, the care with which the peons patted them back into place and tucked the tissue paper lovingly about them so I could close each trunk again somewhat restored my tottering faith in humankind. The day drew to a windy, rainy close and nothing had been accomplished except that I'd caught a horrible cold.

The night did little to restore our equilibrium. We had picked a hotel close to the customs station, but it turned out to be rather colorful. Drunks and tarts played and shouted in the halls all night long, every now and then thumping on our doors and importuning us to come forth and frolic. Border towns! By morning I was in near hysterics, in no condition to renew the fray over my beautiful costumes.

Deciding shrewdly that we could do without the advice of a driver, we hired a car and drove ourselves back and forth over the International Bridge for the hundreds of papers the Mexican officials now demanded we produce. I had obtained my vaccination certificate in Los Angeles. *Muy mal, señorita.* We had thought of getting in a bit of hunting during our stay, so we had brought shotguns. *Absurdo, señorita.* During one of our pauses on the Mexican side one of the under-officials had an idea. Directing me to reveal my shawls again, he selected one, hefted it in first one hand, then the other. "This," he finally said gravely, "will pay ten dollars' duty."

"What?" roared Carreras. "But we are taking it out again! We'll deposit for the lot, but then when we leave, we must have back the money. That is the way every civilized country works it!" I had a sinking feeling the adjective was unfortunate.

"I am sorry," said the official stiffly, "but here it is the law that all silks must pay duty on their weight. I shall have to charge a straight duty on all your costumes. Yes, it is a pity, for there are a good many of them. However, *señor,* I am *muy caballero.* If you were to pay me one hundred pesos, my memory—well, it is not always good."

Fine—at least for the moment. But then the man higher up heard about this little transaction, so he had to be paid—not to tell on us. Even when we finally made our train, two horrible days later, another official who'd heard about it all too late to get in line for his share tracked us aboard our train and collected duty on our battered old gramophone—a 100 percent duty. We reflected sadly as the train pulled out that Mexico was changing with the times.

We arrived at Monterrey at eight in the morning, gave a performance that night, packed after the show, and were off again the next morning. A local official tried, with a zeal worthy a better cause, to shake us down. Unexpectedly, Carreras threatened him with a punch in the nose. Oddly enough, this seemed to work as well as if not better than palm oil.

After one concert in Saltillo we drove on to Torreón over the most barren of deserts. Here were color and line to delight any painter, but with naked mountains frowning down on us and all the cacti and coyotes, we felt glad to be awheel and able to put it behind us. We arrived at Torreó at one, arranged the costumes, something like a traveling salesman setting up goods for the inspection of buyers, and I gave a concert that night.

Our next engagement was in San Luis Potosí. To our dismay we found that neither rail nor motor road connected Torreón and San Luis, and we would have to retrace the unfriendly desert to Saltillo, where people who knew about these things would see that we got to San Luis when the time came.

We stopped at noon for lunch at a combined two-room shack and filling station set forlornly in the barrenness. A fat Mexican señora served us lunch of marvelous rice and black beans. Afterward I asked her for the "ladies' room." With voluble pleasure she conducted me across a half mile of mesquiteless desert to a crack in the tortuously sun-dried earth. We returned to the car gray with dust. Carreras took a picture of us, and we asked her name so that we could send her a print.

"Maria Angela Dolores Menendez de Hernandes y Torres," she rattled off happily. We hoped we'd get it straight when the time came.

We could afford to kill a little time in Saltillo, and when I had faithfully done my daily three hours of practice, I took advantage of the hospitality of the people and went out with them to several local celebrations and parties. It served to introduce me to a conversational gambit universally practiced by young Mexican gentlemen enjoying the years of their great romantic period.

If you believe them, you will find every young Mexican, in the years roughly between his late teens and early thirties, to be a great singer, a great fighter, and a great lover. His family, so he assures you, is of the Spanish aristocracy. He himself has been a bullfighter, a general, a politician, a dancer, and a successful businessman in New York and has made at least one miraculous escape from certain death by swimming the Rio Grande. Such bravura stories I heard with little variation at least half a dozen times in as many places from as many handsome young men.

One of these great-lover, great-fighter youngsters proposed to entertain us with a shooting party. (He informed us casually that he could shoot a bird on the wing at fifty yards with a six-gun from the hip.) Advising us not to be late for our 5 A.M. appointment, he made sure of being on time himself by the simple expedient of not going to bed. By dawn he was unmistakably showing the wear and tear of too much tequila.

We were to go out to the "ranch of my father"—all Mexico belongs to the fathers of these fellows—to shoot wild duck on a huge lake. When we got there, we found there hadn't been a drop of water in that lake for a good two years. Later we ate lunch in the fortified village where the "hands" lived with their families. The inhabitants of the work village were pure Indian. They lived in a great square surrounding the animal corrals. Their mud houses were scarcely weather-worthy, and the single rooms were shared by adults, children, dogs, chickens, and pigs.

With some difficulty they managed to locate four chairs for us. These were gentle, courteous people, shyly anxious to make us comfortable. I shall not soon forget the heavy-graven features and soft voice of the blind man who rode up to the dooryard

where we were eating to make us welcome with a jug of wine.
It seemed to me that it was not our flamboyant young host but
the ancient who was *muy caballero*!

It was an interesting creative sensation to be staying in one
country while preparing dances and ethnic-dance lectures on, for
example, the Orient. Yet here in an atmosphere of lovely old
plazas, balconied houses, strolling guitar players, swaggering,
spurred charros, and pretty girls convoyed home from mass by
vigilant duennas I somehow managed to think and plan in terms
of temple bells and the vastly intricate symbolism underlying
dances of the East.

Considering the complications of getting there, the San Luis
Potosí engagement seemed of laughable brevity. One day, one
concert. Then we made for Mexico City to stay for a month.
In that luxury of time we gave a relatively small number of
concerts—eight to be exact. In this we had the dubious assistance
of a "cold war" going on between Mexico and the United States
over oil concessions.

Yet in spite of the volatile local situation we had many joys
and satisfactions during our stay. Mexico had been the first
Spanish-speaking country in which I had danced, and now again
it was good to hear the "olés!" for the *Alegrías*, the *Farruca,*
and the Ravel *Bolero.*

We went to the bullfights and saw again the great Portuguese
fighter Semao de Veiga and his magnificent mounts. I took lessons in cape work and in Mexican dances that were new to me.
I climbed the pyramids, where I became so dizzy that I had to
descend, backing down on all fours. And I attended a party
given in my honor that was so charming, so sincere, and so Old
World that it touched me. The host was the director of a
private conservatory of music and president of the Bach Society.
The party was in a small hall set back in a tiny garden. When
we drove up, the pupils—something over a hundred of them—
were on the steps and as we entered showered us with carnations. We sat solemnly in a circle while the maestro made a fine,
laudatory speech about me. The pupils shouted six times in
cadence, "Viva La Meri! Viva La Meri!" then presented me with

a huge bouquet. The climax of the tribute was the two-piano performance by the maestro and his prize pupil of the Bach concerto from which my *Madonna* music is taken. I had been entertained many times more elaborately, but the directness and simplicity of this party, its lack of pretense, made it seem a courtesy from a kindlier, more gracious era.

We went on to Guadalajara. There, happily, we could feel ourselves back in Old Mexico with progress and politics left behind. We were met at the station with flowers, and a good portion of the community escorted us to the hotel. We sighed with relief. In the afternoon, driving in an ancient victoria drawn by an equally ancient Rosinante, we went out to the pottery works, where workers were delighted to explain to us the hand manufacture of the famous pieces. I longed to have some of the vases, but they were big enough to hide the Forty Thieves in and too delicate to transport. And with sixty-seven trunks already . . .

Our rest and relaxation did not last through the night. A girl across the street was soon to be married, and her fiancé sent three separate orchestras to serenade her. By taking turns, they managed to make the compliment last the whole night. But the music was beautiful and had a sort of contagion; before dawn I began to feel quite bridey myself.

Six days and two concerts later we left for Manzanillo and the blue, blue sea. We spent a day at the customs, freeing the bond. Although the authorities were most courteous and of "Old Mexico," the process did take time. Later I realized that I should have had a snapshot of us in the customs shed, it was all so characteristic—among our trunks and boxes, waiting for the officials; Carreras, sitting on a suitcase with the typewriter on a trunk, catching up with overdue correspondence and routine matters; I on another trunk, waving my hands vaguely as I mentally choreographed a new dance; Averardo, addressing postcards against a wall; Olivia, notebook on knee, forever verifying her list of my costumes and accessories. This was always the time for doing our "homework."

But at last even the customs officials came to the end of what they could do, and we went aboard the southbound *Heiyo Maru*. Like the Japanese themselves, the ship was phenomenally clean. The combination of clean ship and clean ship's complement was something to bring peace to the soul.

South America and the School of Natya

In May 1938 we were in Lima. The concert given on my birth-day proved especially exciting. We had already given six concerts in the National Theatre, wonderfully successful, and this one would close my season.

It was a "vermouth" concert, meaning that it began at 6:30 P.M., because the Limenian dines near midnight and, so far as I know, never goes to bed at all. The concert was presented by the Japanese ambassador. He took the theater, contracted the artist, and opened the doors to the large Japanese colony, all in the interest of culture, because, as he told me, many young Japanese in the colony had been born in Peru and had never seen Japanese dancing. Therefore he requested me to present my entire Japanese repertoire.

Naturally it is particularly satisfying to perform ethnic dances for those to whose culture they belong, and in this case I had the further joy of knowing I was actually introducing these dances to many in my audience.

Even my familiar dressing room looked a little unfamiliar to me that evening, for every hanger held a kimono of rich, multi-colored silk, and ranged along the dressing table were my masks and elaborate wigs, mutely challenging me to do my best. For my feet there waited not heels or pink ballet shoes and bells but a battalion of pristine white *tabi*. A challenge but also a joy, since for one whole program the body, the spirit, and the heart could express themselves through a single movement language. From the all-important spinal line each muscle responds within the frame of a single style, and the emotional impetus finds its outlet through a single dynamic response.

During *Genroku Hanami Odori,* a spring dance, children
posted in upper boxes showered me with thousands of pink rose
petals. When the last number finished, a serious little butterfly
child in full Japanese costume presented a huge basket of blooms
and a pair of dancing fans.

In the greenroom I received the congratulations of the older
generation and signed autographs for the youngsters. They spoke
Japanese, Spanish, English, yet only I and the flower bearer in
all that crowd wore Japanese dress. Weary yet exalted, I took
off my makeup while Olivia hung up my exotic silks and
smoothed my precious wigs.

When we returned to the hotel, the maître d'hôtel ushered
me into a small dining room, where I was met with the Limenian
"brindisi"—a crescendo of applause to a percussion of table-
pounding fingers—led by the great critic Carlos Raygada. A
group of friends sat around the table, whose centerpiece was a
huge birthday cake! It was a wonderful party. We toasted each
other in good red wine—I toasting the critics, the critics toasting
me. Then gifts were presented to me—gifts from artists and
writers, musicians and journalists; gifts of heavy Peruvian silver
and colorful Andean wools. It made a birthday I shall never
forget!

Chile too received me as a valued friend. I was showered
with gifts, entertained at parties. How we danced the cueca,
handkerchiefs snapping and flying in our hands, our feet tingling
with banquet champagne!

In ten days I gave five concerts and then, at the request of
the Bellas Artes, a series of conferences on various aspects of
ethnic dance. It was during a lecture-demonstration on Spanish
dancing that the totally unexpected occurred.

The conferences were given in the Bellas Artes Hall. The
rear section had been laced with scaffolding erected for the
cleaning of the frescoes. The audiences were so large that many
students perched on the scaffolding. I was in the midst of the
Goyescas when there was an untoward clatter from the hitherto
most attentive audience. Glancing up, I saw students tumbling
from their perch. An earth tremor! I somehow went on with

my dance; the students calmly clambered back, and again the audience concentrated on watching me, quite unmoved by this hiccough by nature.

I do not envy the folk who cross the Andes by air. It is true, one gains much comfort on wings, but, too, one misses much of beauty.

We left Santiago by rail at 8 P.M., arriving at Los Andes at 1:40, and were off again after a very short night's sleep. The mountains were truly magnificent. The last time I had seen them it had been full summer; this time they were clad in the snows of midwinter and even lovelier. Inca Lake was frozen over; Aconcagua was wreathed in clouds and mist; Inca Bridge spanned a waterfall of icicles.

At one o'clock we descended from the train at Las Vacas. It seemed that a mountain had crashed down on the railway line and we must proceed by car. In a fleet of Fords we negotiated a narrow gravel trail and hairpin curves at hair-raising speeds. It was a frightening experience but well worth it, for it gave us a rare view of the awesome high Andes. Descending from the car, shaky, banged up but in one piece, we stopped for tea at an Argentinian inn and watched the gauchos on their stocky, woolly horses herd cattle through the town. A bit later, again by train, we crossed the pampas into Buenos Aires.

We had planned to pass through Buenos Aires and go on immediately to Montevideo. But the day of our arrival in the Argentinian metropolis was a national holiday, hence for three days no baggage would be handled. Perforce, then, we went to a hotel. And what happened? We never got to Montevideo at all.

To amuse ourselves during our enforced visit we called on old friends, so word got around that we were in town. The Wagnerian Society asked me to give a conference at the Odeon Theatre. Then since that had drawn a full house, the Odeon management contracted for three concerts.

Buenos Aires is a difficult city to conquer, so a success there is doubly satisfying; all went marvelously well. For me the experience was heightened because a decade earlier I had made no very deep impression on this city. I was expecting, at

least from the critics, an echo of their former coolness. Not at
all! Only one critic, recalling his doubts of my '28 season, wrote
that "having seen both Argentina and La Meri in their formative
years, Buenos Aires had failed to discern the genius of either."
My reaction was that as long as he bracketed me with Argentina,
he could say anything else about me he pleased!

We were leaving shortly for Italy and home, so in the interval before our sailing date we went for a three-day shoot in
Chascomús. It would have been unthinkable—almost heresy—to
have circled the world with a trunkful of shooting gear, including
three shotguns and a rifle, and then not use them in Argentina,
that paradise of hunters.

At dawn on the morning of August 10 we walked up the
gangplank, really bound for Italy! It seemed too good to be
true. My mind was alive with anticipation. Would Booch remember me? How much would the pines have grown? How
would the Mediterranean look? All across the sunny Atlantic I
sang with joy. Twenty-seven months ago we had left Italy. Our
lives since then had been filled to overflowing with the richness
of work and study in eighteen different lands. Replete, I longed
now for the relaxation of sleeping in my own bed in a room
where no luggage sat staring at me.

In six days we docked at Genoa and at once boarded a
train for Campolecciano. I ran from window to window like a
mad thing, not to miss a single familiar sight along the way.
Sunny, quiet, smiling, like a Renaissance painting, the country
slipped by. I demanded of Olivia that she tell me every one of
her first impressions—and was far too excited to listen to any of
her answers. At Livorno we hired a car to drive the seventeen
kilometers of winding sea road to our home. We turned in
through the big iron gates.

Ah yes, the dark pines *had* grown. The vines and olive
trees were heavy with fruit. Sun dappled the rambling white
stone house, holding out to us a rich welcome of peace. Along
the drive came Booch, ears flapping, rear end in hysterical
spasms of welcome. No, she had not forgotten me. Her serious
little white face, framed by the long black ears, was alight with

joyful recognition. Everything, including siren Mediterranean,
welcomed us home.

In these Elysian fields we took a two-month vacation. The
sea was calm as a millpond. We went swimming every day, row-
ing the *patino* far out and diving off its bobbing decks. We took
long walks in the hills, bicycled to all the surrounding towns.
We shot clay pigeons from our boathouse roof by the sea while
Booch and her son, Wop, exhausted themselves trying to retrieve
the broken disks.

The theater never, never bestows a complete vacation.
Daily practice must go on, always a strict necessity. Our costumes had to be refurbished, our records relabeled. But when
the work could be done on the wide terrace above the sea, it
seemed less a chore than a pastoral game.

In November we were ready to do concerts and lecture
demonstrations in Florence, Rome, and Naples. In the capital,
after I had spoken on the eastern dance arts and demonstrated
with six Oriental dances in full and authentic costume, a charming grande dame came backstage. "You spoke so well and
taught us so much, my dear," she said, "and now, where are the
six little ladies who danced for you? I want to tell them how
much I enjoyed them too." I had some difficulty convincing
her that all six little ladies were I.

Christmas at home was in the old-fashioned American tradition. We went into the hills and cut our tree. Our gifts were
homemade and tagged with amusing verses. Our *contadino*
neighbors came in for a sip from the wassail bowl, and we had a
great turkey dinner. It was a lovely, lovely Christmas. I closed
my ears to the rumbling of submarines in my blue sea and my
eyes to cries of *"Tire dirètto"* in the newspapers.

In January 1939 we left for London, and I never saw my
Italian home—or my beloved Booch—again.

In London I gave a week of daily performances at the Duke
of York's Theatre. I should have been very happy, for it was
good to return to a London audience and to see Stocky and his
lovely wife, Ginger, again. Over festive colas we three old friends
talked long and late in the pink-taffeta dressing room, which had

just been redecorated for Markova's engagement. But a cloud
lay heavy across the world, so heavy that it penetrated even my
art-insulated consciousness. All mankind was marching stubborn-
ly toward a tragic destiny, and we felt an odd psychic need to
hurry and live normally while normal living was yet possible. As
though to some temperamental giant orchestra, I danced
frenetically against the ominous accompaniment.

Early in February we crossed an angry North Atlantic.
Seas broke unceasingly over the decks; every rope was frozen
within a tube of ice. Tempo was quickening and it was as
though this sea change were affecting all things in our changing
world.

We plunged immediately into the Columbia Concerts tour,
opening at the St. James Theatre in New York. Olivia, returning
to San Antonio, was replaced by Carreras's niece, Juana. The
tour was different from any I had hitherto known. The once
friendly "seasons" were replaced by endless one-night stands.
Only one thing remained constant: Lilian joined me for the
tour. We traveled in a chauffeured Cadillac, which pulled a
trailer carrying the luggage. I cannot remember what cities we
played, for the trip fused into a frenzied fantasy of arrivals,
shows, departures. I contracted a virus and too often danced
with a temperature of 104.

Two months and eight states later we returned to New
York, only to ship immediately for Caracas. I was glad to go,
for I wanted to escape into the world I had known, a world of
sunny peace. Alas, Caracas too had changed. Gone were the
quiet houses of pink adobe; in their place was arising, noisily, a
modern, western metropolis.

As flying was out of the question for us, we had to go to
Trinidad to await a boat that would take us to our next engagement in Rio. On this tropic Carib isle life moved much as it
always had. I should have found some balm on the golden
beaches. But global tensions were in the air and I danced in an
ominous passion of speed. Any creative artist brings to the stage
all that is his innermost self. Discriminating eyes in an audience
can, in one short evening, know an artist better than do dearest

friends. Up to now I had danced always "in the sun" out of the pure joy of living. How that amazing instrument of the body reacts to the workings of the mind! Muscles and sinews, schooled for years to strict discipline, can, influenced by the dark moods of the mind, become utterly unreliable. And so it was with me.

At a concert in Rio one night I gave my ankle a bad wrench. We had to cancel the performance. Weeping, I was taken to the hotel in a taxi, my whole lower leg swollen to the size of a watermelon. The house doctor looked at it, told me there might be a break, strongly advised a specialist's attention and an X ray in the morning. For two weeks I was in a cast. Engagements in Rio were, *per forza,* canceled, and I whiled away the long hours, bereft of even practicing, by starting on a book about the gesture language of Indian dance.

A little shaky, but on my two feet at last, we concertized in Pôrto Alegre and went on down to Montevideo for a season there.

In Montevideo there came backstage one evening "Indio Bravo." This was the pen name of a strikingly handsome woman from Madrid who was a critic on an important daily. She looked very gitana with her slick ebony hair and slim body. She asked me to give her a little red comb from my gypsy costume. Surprised, I complied. She thrust it into her hair. "You see, I already wear two others. This one is from Argentina and this one from Pastora. So now you join them. I have seen many Spanish dancers and I shall see many more. Yet it is long that I have worn only two combs and I think it will again be long before I wear four."

How infinitely proud she made me! Even when I put away my *bata* and slipped into my street dress, my head was held as high as that of any Andalusian.

We had given only a few performances in Buenos Aires when all-out war was declared in Europe. With all plans and the usual patterns of living disrupted, Europeans fought for passage on the last boats home. In a matter of hours we, too, had to make big decisions. I had two homes, heart roots in two

far-separated lands. But in this desperate moment I discovered
that I had only *one* country.

Several days later we stepped aboard the S.S. *Argentina,*
bound for New York. Though the boat was crowded with interesting people, among them many celebrities—Elman, Brailow-
sky, Schipa—it was a sad trip. As though nature herself shared
our confusion, typhoons knocked us about in the Caribbean.
The talk was all of war, of our abandoned homes in Europe.
My own heart was as empty and full of melancholy as a theater
after the show is over and only the work light burns on the
stage.

For four months after our return to the States we went on
with concert engagements, but transportation was rapidly becoming unpredictable due to the war. Engagements dropped off
gradually too. So it was not only pleasant but providential that,
with Dave teaching at New York University, he and Lilian were
living in the city and had a guest room! Carreras and I moved
in with them, while Juana stayed in a nearby hotel. We took a
small studio on the west side where our theater material could
be stored and I could carry on my daily three-hour rehearsals.

Irene Lewisohn asked me to give a lecture on Indian dance
and costume at the Museum of Costume Arts. I had become
fairly acclimated to public speaking and it was pleasant to be
able to speak in English to English-speaking people.

Scarcely was the lecture over when a beautiful tall woman,
all in black, a huge picture hat setting off her white hair, burst
into my dressing room. She embraced me with vigor and
stepped back to survey me, augmenting the brilliance of her eyes
with large gestures. "My dear!" she cried. "I will not take no
for an answer; I simply will not! You *must* open a school! Together we will found a center for the study of eastern arts—
dancing, painting, sculpture, philosophy! America is hungry for
this. And only you can give it!"

I tried to mutter that I did not want to teach, but my
visitor was in full cry and did not even hear me.

"Do you realize the fount of knowledge you can bring to
your country?" she demanded. "The generations of youth you

Krishna Gopala (Choreography, La Meri; music, Vishnu Dass Shirali). (*Left to right*) Lillian Rollo, Rebecca Harris, Juana Carreras, Edna Dieman, La Meri (as Krishna), Patty Page, Lilian Newcomer, and Marilyn Duberstein. Debut, 1940. (Photo taken on-stage La Meri's E.D.C. theater on East 59th Street, New York City)

Carabali (Cuba). (Photo: Rosel, New York, 1944)

El Gato (Argentina). (Photo: Rosel, New York, 1944)

Marwari Kathak (Choreography, Ram Dutt Misra). (Photo: Rosel, New York, 1944)

Zandunga (Mexico). (Photo: Rosel, New York, 1944)

Sign- talk Songs (Amerind). Photo: Rosel, New York, 1944)

Farruca. (Photo: Marcus Blechman, New York, 1944)

Nasu to Kabocha (Choreography, Kodera). (Photo: Marcus Blechman, New York, 1945)

Serimpi (Java). (Photo: Marcus Blechman, New York, 1946)

Song of Songs (Choreography, Ted Shawn; music, Manuel Galea) at Jacob's Pillow, 1951. (*Left to right*) Peter Di Falco, La Meri, and Ted Shawn. (Photo: Jack Mitchell)

Huayno (Peru). (Photo: Marcus Blechman, New York, 1949)

La Meri and Peter Di Falco in *Yaravi* (Choreography, La Meri) at Jacob's Pillow, 1948. (Photo: John
van Lund)

can feed with the knowledge of the savant and the fire of the artist? I have it all worked out. You will take a studio in the building where I am—there is one vacancy, just below me—and all I want is to sit at your feet and, at long last, learn the true technique of the eastern dance!" She paused for breath. "By the way, I am Ruth St. Denis," she said absently.

I truly did not want to teach. I did not want to open a school. But I was to find out that Miss Ruth had not become a living legend for nothing. She was a torrent of embodied enthusiasm, as easy to avoid as a hurricane. Perhaps she was right; perhaps America *was* actually hungering for knowledge and therefore might be persuaded to pay a living wage to receive it. Thinking practically, I well knew that, so few were engagements now, we were very close to living off my sister and her husband, a situation that continually distressed my conscience.

So by mid-May we had taken two giant steps—that is, relatively speaking. We had moved into the studio below Miss Ruth's, where, though cramped, there were basic living quarters for all four of us; we had opened The School of Natya.

My very first pupil was the already nationally known Jack Cole, who came for a series of private lessons. Not only was he a charming gentleman, he was the hardest-working student I have ever had.

One hoped, of course, that this would set the tone of the new venture, be an omen of success for the future. But it did not take long to discover that very few young dancers, indeed, were able to pay for lessons. Though my rates were far from unreasonable, the only thing to do was cut them down and, in cases of talented and sincerely ambitious youngsters, to give scholarships.

The device that really floated the school (and us) financially was a thing we called reunions. Weekly, on Tuesday evening, for an admission fee of seventy-five cents, Miss Ruth or I would give a demonstration lecture and as our pupils began to make progress, a full dance program.

In July Mary Washington Ball, at that time head of the Jacob's Pillow Summer Dance School near Lee, Massachusetts, engaged me for a lecture-demonstration and a performance.

I returned to New York to find that in my absence Miss Ruth and Carreras had decided to give an "evening" at the Kaufmann Auditorium. And Miss Ruth was going to dance!

We should have known it would be a historic occasion, and it was, for Miss Ruth had not danced on the stage for many years, and she still had a public that was dithering to see her once again.

The program was built on solos designed to be a sort of expository counterpoint. First I would do the classical version of a dance, say, of India or Java; Miss Ruth would then do her own romantic version of the same dance. As she explained it in her opening speech, "La Meri will do these dances as they have been done for centuries in the land of their origin. Then I will do them as I darn well please."

She was absolutely wonderful to work with. Though I felt she loved me and wanted me to succeed, there was, nevertheless, a sense of competition between us that made each of us work to give the very best performance possible.

Reams have been written about Ruth St. Denis as an artist. Let me forever record from my experience that she was a stanch and unwavering friend, that kind of "very present help in time of trouble" who never fails to find the answers to calm an overwrought soul in the travail of artistic creation. Apart from her immortal personal artistry, it was my happy experience to find her a tremendous woman.

As mentioned previously, during my enforced layoff in Rio I had started a book on India's gesture language. There is a temptation to suppose that a book, since it comes out of the mind, can be written wherever and whenever one can sit down for a few minutes. I have found that something of a myth, to say the least. Columbia University, through the intervention of Marguerite Block, curator of the Bush Oriental Collection, now asked me to complete the book for publication.

At least I found out what can be achieved by shutting out sound and concentrating. I moved to a hotel where I could have uninterrupted quiet and in five days of writing ten hours a day finished the manuscript and took it up to the university. The

two hundred illustrations were duly made from photographs.
Dr. Ananda K. Coomaraswamy, after looking at the text, agreed
to write the foreword. Dr. Heinrich Zimmer, eminent Sanskrit
scholar, corrected the Sanskrit interpolations and wrote an introduction. By spring the book was off the press.

Life brought me another big dividend that spring in my
friendships with Argentinita and Pilar Lopez. They had come to
one of our Spanish "reunions." As we talked afterward, we discovered an instant mutual sympathy.

Like Ruth St. Denis, Argentinita had her share of beautiful
rewards and deserved praise for her artistry. As a human being,
she was a great lady and a devoted scholar, uncompromisingly
dedicated to her art—very different from being uncompromisingly
dedicated to oneself as an artist! We talked long hours on the
history and motivations of Spanish dancing, and sometimes she
would drop in on a Natya Dancers' rehearsal and take a hand in
teaching my awe-struck youngsters *coplas* of the sevillanas or the
jota.

My Natya Dancers were, indeed, becoming quite well known.
At the Needle Trades Series, Pearl Buck's *East and West Evenings,* and the American Museum of Natural History we gave
concerts featuring full Indian ballets of my devising. My girls
were young and very, very pretty. That they were genuinely
talented is proved by the fact that nearly all of them went on to
national and international reputations.

By late summer Carreras had decided that our living in the
studio was ridiculously impossible. We went hunting in New
Jersey for a house to rent. The Master Institute had offered me
rent-free studios for my classes plus a well-equipped theater for
performances, so it seemed logical to expect that we could make
enough to pay the rent of a house. Carreras disliked New York
with a passion, and I myself was far from averse to seeing a tree
growing now and then.

We moved to Montclair in the fall. Three times a week I
caught an eight o'clock bus to spend all day teaching and return,
after evening classes, at eleven at night. My teaching days were
so full that I ate lunch and supper while I taught.

The other four days of the week I spent at home, vibrating
between housekeeping and the endless writing of notebooks and
the organizing of teaching techniques. Right here let me say I
never cooked. Carreras was not only a gourmet but, happily for
our digestions, a cordon bleu. So, however tough the financial
going might be at any given moment, our meals were Lucullan.
Thus, since I never set foot in the kitchen except under protest,
when I say "housekeeping," I mean cleaning, dusting, and
scrubbing out the bathtub. I rationalize my feeling about this
by assuring myself that anything that has to be done over and
over again is futile. One paints a picture or creates a ballet and
it is *done*, complete in itself.

When we made the move, it seemed financially perfectly
plausible. But we reckoned without pampered New York audiences. The audiences that had gladly packed our studios in
Tenth Street simply declined to make the trek up to 113th
Street. Performances, which had always floated the school, fell
off at the box office until the wolf made himself heard distinctly,
snuffling around the door.

Beatrice Kraft, one of the loveliest of my Natya Dancers,
had left to join Jack Cole. The other girls set up a kitty into
which we put every spare penny to help defray the expense of
costumes. Nevertheless, things kept sliding downward. Just
when it seemed that they had reached the possible worst, Lilian
and I got a firm cash offer for the San Antonio home. It was
heartbreakingly low, but I was desperate, and Lilian consented
to the sale. So for a time we managed to keep going.

The Natya Dancers were very much in demand—not so
much for paid performances as for appearances at educational in-
stitutions. We still had our little Ford truck, so we could carry
girls and costumes to engagements. Artistically we were a rousing success; financially, an abysmal failure. That was to be
somewhat the story of my life in New York. Lilian would come
up from Fort Belvoir often to dance with us and help make costumes. But soon even this moral support was denied me by the
Army, which ordered Dave to Kansas at midsummer.

I do not know the name of the kind woman in Montclair

who gave me my dog, Topsy. I wish I did, for the little cross-bred puppy, result of My Own Brucie's playing Romeo to a Welsh terrier Juliet, was to prove my constant companion for seventeen years. So many other players who have their entrances and their exits in these pages have disappeared into limbo or been absorbed into lives of their own. Sometimes dogs are my favorite people!

Ted Shawn, founder and again director of Jacob's Pillow, invited the Natya Dancers up for Hindu Week. It meant daily teaching and two performances in the newly built theater. So for transportation we bought an old secondhand Buick for $165, and with that and the truck we took our material and girls to the Berkshires.

Shawn had engaged Argentinita for Spanish Week, but Encarna had told him she would not teach and had suggested that I teach in her place. So I went up again and had the joy of being reunited with Encarna, Pilar, and their new partner, Federico Rey.

For August Carreras had gotten us a season at the Hunterton Hills Playhouse in New Jersey. For five weeks we put on weekly performances, spending our days in lessons and swimming in the pool. Nature was beautiful and our group suffered no more from quarrels than any large family of individualists. When the cook quit, Carreras took over in the kitchen, making mealtimes salubrious affairs.

It was obvious that financially we could not survive in a studio on 113th Street, so before the Hunterton Hills engagement terminated, I jumped down to New York to seek out a new location. At last I found one suited to our lean circumstances on a top floor on 46th Street just off Fifth Avenue. Interestingly enough the lower floors were occupied by Fred LeQuorne, in whose studio I had given my first audition for Carreras. I signed a lease. The landlord was wonderful to us and gave us furniture and mirrors from his vast store. Carreras and Averardo went to work to build platforms for our eventual public and to plan a schedule of guest speakers.

The roster of honored guests for our "reunions" in that

studio reads like a *Who's Who*: Pearl Buck, Lin Yutang, Krishnalal Shridharani, Argentinita, Ruth St. Denis, Ted Shawn, Sarkis Katchadourian, Felix Cleve, Marguerite Block . . .

Suddenly we discovered we were actually making money! In a browned-out city our 75-cent admissions were packing them in!

Because I commuted daily by now-irregular buses, I often flopped down and stayed overnight in the studio. Fifth Avenue in the brownout was an eerie section, a deserted city within a deserted city. One could walk a twenty-block mile and see not one human soul other than the dim shapes within a ghostly police car. Yet there was something about the forbidding loneliness that I loved. It gave me the feeling that in the whole world there was only I to meet, with whatever strength I possessed, that darkling danger lying in wait at the next shadowy doorway.

One memorable day was spent with Ananda K. Coomaraswamy when he came down from Boston to give a lecture at the Waldorf. At the end of the lecture I was to do a dance. With Dr. Coomaraswamy sitting in judgment, I was suffocatingly determined to dance well. To my horror I discovered that the "stage" on which I was dancing was constructed of a number of collapsible tables lashed together with utmost indifference. In the evening of that same day Dr. Coomaraswamy and I did a dual broadcast, and it heartened me to feel that in the eyes of an undisputed cognoscente of my art I had succeeded.

The Natyas began to display a hunger for knowledge of the cultural backgrounds of the arts they were practicing, so I laid out a summer course of master classes for the study of these backgrounds. The lectures were open to the public, and I was tremendously encouraged when Carola Goya and Ruth Anderson of the Iberian Institute came to attend the Spanish section.

We could not blink at the fact that war activities were cutting into our progress—in performances, pupils, income—even though we were the only remaining dance activity still working outside the commercial field. In our area of diminishing returns I was teaching nine hours a day to the certain neglect of my own dancing.

Miss Ruth, who had moved into Isadora Duncan's old studio on East 59th Street, called me one day to say that she was going to California for good. "I want you to come to my studio," she said, "and select whichever of my group costumes you can use. I want to leave them with you." It was thrilling encouragement.

Carreras, Averardo, and I went over in the truck. The studio occupied a whole floor and had two very large rooms, two baths, and several smaller rooms. Carreras was at once—and vocally—in love with it, envisioning a stage built at the end of one of the larger rooms. The 46th Street studio had at least gallantly supported us, and perhaps I should not have let myself be carried away. But the mere thought of a real stage to work on instead of the curtained-off floor of a hall was just too much for me. We took over Miss Ruth's lease and prepared to move in. Carreras tracked down two "angels" to lend the money for stage construction and necessary redecoration, and he and Averardo pitched into the arduous work of construction.

Since studio work was impossible while this was going on, I went up to Jacob's Pillow for two weeks of teaching and performing, thence to Kansas for a two-week visit with my sister and her husband.

We opened our little dance theater in the early fall. Of our 110 seats few were ever unoccupied, and after each performance the large salon was filled with distinguished and appreciative people, many of them refugees from the war in Europe.

The American Museum of Natural History was running a series of ethnic-dance concerts, and we played in that auditorium on an average of twice a month. We continued our own policy of weekly reunions. I certainly had all the work I could either desire or do.

In January of 1944 in a casual conversation on dance with the noted ballet authority Anatole Chujoy I came up with the idea of doing *Swan Lake* in Indian techniques. Mr. Chujoy was enthusiastic and gave me incalculable help by showing me the classic choreography.

This was my first public step away from the purely authentic in dance and I became completely engrossed in it. Without stopping either classes or regular performances, we went into a new welter of costume making and rehearsing. Lilian's husband was ordered overseas, so she came to live in New York. Taking the penthouse in our building, she saved her own sanity by immersing herself in every facet of my work.

We presented *Swan Lake* in February of 1944, and it was not only a succès d'estime but a respectable practical success as well. The critics gave us glowing reviews, and many of the classical Swan Queens, among them Alexandra Danilova, from whom I still treasure a letter praising our presentation, came to view this iconoclastic version of their ballet.

There was also tragedy in my personal life in 1944. Carreras and I separated with a good deal of drama and nervous tension. My sister's husband was killed in France; I had loved him like a brother. But work is the only panacea for sorrow, and we worked fourteen hours a day.

The mission of a performing artist is to bring joy and beauty—escape, if you will—to his audience. The mission of a teacher is education in the highest sense. The personal travail of an artist or teacher is his own burden and he has no right to unload his heartaches on the public.

"I count only the hours that shine."

The Ethnologic Dance Center

All my life—and I was now forty-six—someone else had handled the finances, first my parents and then Carreras. Mathematics, even in its most primitive form, has always eluded me, and I still count on my fingers. I added to my other chores my own sort of bookkeeping, but after a year of utter confusion I called in a C.P.A., Sam Prussak, to sort things out. The expression on this young man's face when he confronted my "books" was a study in drama. But he got it all sorted out—and has kept me sorted out ever since.

I had announced *El Amor Brujo* for the theater, but Carreras, who had mimed the role of the Ghost in my earlier presentation, was no longer available, so I began looking for a male dancer with a Spanish dance background.

I knew nothing whatever about the young man who presented himself, but he had the right height and the right look, and he had studied dance, so we went into immediate rehearsal.

The night before the opening, in the midst of a late, long rehearsal, a policeman appeared. Flushed with our labors, our practice clothes wilted, we stood in a circle, transfixed by the sight of the tall, taciturn figure in the blue uniform. He mumbled something about doing his duty and produced a warrant for the arrest of my new dancer. He left, taking our Ghost with him. As the door closed behind them with finality, the studio was in an uproar.

"Oh, Madame La Meri, will we have the show?"

"Maybe you'd better call Mr. Carreras!"

"Couldn't we do *Swan Lake* instead?"

"Why don't we just cancel the performance?"

159

"Oh, be quiet and go home!" I cried. "We shall have the show as scheduled!" Chastened, they quietly went away. I sat on the floor, head in hands, groping for a way out.

Once I'd got my mind organized, it proved not so difficult. Though it was late at night, I phoned my old friend, Juan de Beaucaire-Montalvo. He had grown fat with age after his retirement, but he knew the music and the story and he had been a great Spanish dancer in his youth. Though I did not know it, he had retired because of a bad heart. When I begged him to jump in and do the role, he accepted, making the condition that he have only a one-hour rehearsal. It seemed impossible on the face of it. Yet at the opening the following night he went unerringly through the ballet, giving the Ghost an exceptionally fine dramatic interpretation.

Early in November I had a call from Juan Montalvo's assistant, who asked me to emcee a fiesta that Juan had announced and that illness made impossible for him to attend. I was most happy to do this for my old friend, and his party went off pleasantly enough. A week later Juan died. Because of his weak heart his physician had advised him long ago to give up wine, cigarettes, and dancing.

"What?" he had cried. "Without these one is not living at all!" And so he had continued to go his way.

What a gallant hidalgo, this "Spanish" gentleman! A noble representative of a romantic era of the theater now long past, he wore genuine emeralds as studs in his extravagant stage costumes and he chartered planes to visit his lady loves. He was the trusted friend of all the great Spanish dancers, from Amalia Molina to Carmen Amaya. Yet this tall, handsome man with the tiny Latin feet had been born a simple German boy in Brooklyn!

Trained in the hard school of my "stock company" of weekly-change performances, many of my best dancers were leaving for regular employment. My two youngest Natya "children," Nila and Carol, left, the former for the José Greco company, the latter for USO touring. My leading male dancer left to join a musical comedy. I have never wanted to tie my dancers to me to the detriment of their own careers, so I

wished them all the luck in the world and turned back to my
own work.

The summer of 1944 was crowded with an intensive course
in ethnic dance forms that brought us a number of out-of-town
teachers. Lilian and I, with the help of my remaining Natyas,
taught eight hours every day. The summer months also were
punctuated with weekend performances at Jacob's Pillow.

While my spoken and danced production of Tagore's
Chitra was still drawing audiences, I began choreographing
Scheherazade. This ballet was beset with complications. I conceived it in three acts as a full evening's program and for my
theme followed not the ballet libretto but the descriptive notes
of the composer. There was no money for costumes. We
scrambled through the costume room, begged ancient costumes
from blessed Miss Ruth, ripped, sewed, fitted, and finagled.
Lilian, thank heaven, was a marvelous seamstress, and I have a
sort of desperate imagination that can always get something cut
out of nothing. I went down with flu—again—but piled the
costumes on my bed and went on stitching. With a high fever I
crawled out and went on the stage to dance in the opening
performance.

That production, which seemed so ill-fated, was one of the
spiritual high points of my hard years in New York, for a good
friend brought Mr. and Mrs. Fritz Kreisler to our debut performance, and I heard later from his wife that the great violinist
had gone home and sat at the piano half the night, improvising
Oriental melodies, so caught was he by our presentation.

For over a month I was in and out of bed. I had no time
to really get myself well, for there were continual productions at
my theater as well as TV shows, museum shows, and other outside engagements here and there. Besides, I was hard at work on
a new production of Debussy's *Iberia,* a work that called for
sixteen dancers.

Summer wore on. Since our audiences were made up largely of enthusiasts who faithfully attended every new program, I
changed the program each week and created new works on the
average of two a month. Each premiere necessitated new

costumes and long rehearsals, and all the while my classes, day-time and evening, went on. I staged a Caribbean group work called *Voodoo Moon*; I reworked the *Hawaiinuiakea*; I invited as guest artists Dafora, Tei Ko, Tai Ai-Lien and others; I went to the Pillow for my usual weeks of performing and teaching; and on request I staged a full evening of Near Eastern dances.

When it was impossible to get a new show on with the group, I would give solo performances of new works and my *Gesture Songs*, Strauss's *Salome,* and *Press Book,* in which I revived dances from the very start of my career. I was averaging about four hours' sleep in twenty-four, and in September I cracked sufficiently to commit the theatrically heinous crime of throwing a show. In a fit of what the layman calls temperament but we theater folk know is overwork I posted a notice that there would be no performance that night and that theater and school were "closed until further notice."

This foolish outburst cost me two more of my faithful Natyas, and a week later I was back doing the same thing all over again—classes, rehearsals, shows, costumes.

Arthur Miller, one of Montalvo's friends, had gotten us a number of out-of-town engagements, and these added to the bank account and to the general confusion as well. Our old Ford station wagon plowed through sleet and snow to get us west of Chicago and back, south to Carolina and back, north to Boston and back. We had only to set a date for our departure and the weatherman victimized us!

Every cent I made on the road—and it was not much, for I was too desperate to hold out for high fees—went into the seemingly insatiable maw of the Ethnologic Dance Center. And I shudder to think how often Lilian threw what money she could muster into the same cause.

Even to my improvident mind it was obvious that it was not the school but the road work and the theater that were paying the bills. So I determined to replace my dwindling company with new scholarship students and form the Exotic Ballet Company. To this end I offered three G.I. scholarships and also auditioned a number of girls. Dancers, God bless them, are always so hungry to dance! My active theater was a powerful magnet, and I had no trouble selecting fine talents from among the young people who auditioned for the scholarships.

So in January of 1946 the Exotic Ballet Company, with a floating personnel of fifteen, eased into being. Rehearsals became more hectic than ever, for the new group lacked the communal spirit that had made the Natyas so easy to work with. Since temperaments and rivalries were rife, a good deal of my time was spent in soothing ruffled feelings and drying tears. To hold some of my dancers I started paying salaries, although, to my everlasting admiration, there were several who refused payment on the ground that they were receiving lessons and intensive experience and felt they were already being compensated. Then these art-hungry and egotistic children, blind to the fact that I was already overworked as to be on the verge of collapse, demanded lessons in the theories of ethnic dance. Did I refuse? Not I! I have not that kind of common sense. I was so delighted that they wanted to learn that I added background lectures to my already overcrowded schedule.

During the winter and spring of 1946 the Exotic Ballet Company went on the road, driving miles through the inevitable winter weather. The shows were a great success with our audiences in spite of the tensions backstage. I was walking such a fine line financially that I dared not stand up to rebellion. If one of my dancers refused outright to dance a certain role, I would take a hasty glimpse into an overcrowded future, calculate the horror of breaking in someone new, and "eat crow." This, of course, did nothing to improve discipline, nor did it add to my peace of mind. But having fallen in love with the roses, I had to take the thorns with them.

Early in May we presented my *Bach-Bharata Suite*. This was an abstract work using Hindu techniques for the interpretation of certain Bach compositions. Hearing of this East-West fusion, both musicians and dancers were somewhat skeptical. But, I am proud to say, each and every one capitulated when they saw the work.

The press preview was something! I entrusted the mixing

of the cocktails to my ex-G.I. students. I should have known
better! By the time the curtain went up, press and public alike
were feeling no pain! Onstage we dancers, conscious of the
seriousness of the occasion, waited nervously, garbed in austere
black and gold. Bach's "Chorale" commenced, the curtains
parted, and I could almost see the vapors of the martinis wreath-
ing the stage. Such deafening applause I have seldom heard, nor
such enthusiastic bravos. Walter Terry to this day claims he
went back again just to assure himself that he had seen what he
thought he saw through that fine alcoholic haze.

For my next press preview I served tea!

It had now been two years since I had left the protection of
my husband's theatrical know-how to stand on my own feet.
Within limits I had proved myself capable of self-support and of
creating and producing on my own. True, my personal expenses
were austere in the extreme. I lived in an office-bedroom in the
studio; I had scarcely time to eat, and often I did not set foot
out of my domain for days at a time. The financial problem
was not so much that of feeding and housing me as the tail-end
chase of making enough from one production to stage the next.
Yet I managed to solve this problem somewhat by the expedient
of a constant hurricane of endless work.

In the beginning the work and worry had taken up all my
mind and energy. Gradually I grew accustomed to it and began
seeking momentary release from the bitter-sweet joy of creation.
With no realization of the implications I came full circle, picking
up my offstage life where I had laid it down on meeting Carreras
in 1925. Frenetically I took up smoking and cocktails and as-
siduous nightclubbing. Every night after the curtain went down
in my theater, I rushed out on the town, gleefully squired by
men of any and all ages, any and all financial brackets. For a
little while it was a delicious never-never land and I was as happy
as a subdeb.

In the summer of 1946 Shawn engaged the Exotic Ballet as
resident company for the Pillow's summer theater. I could not
afford to close my school entirely, so my sister and I ran between
the Berkshires and New York, at times almost succeeding in

being in two places at once. I took typewriter and reference
books to the Pillow with every intention of writing a book on
Spanish dancing that had been commissioned by A.S. Barnes
and Company. Alas for my good intentions, for the Pillow
proved even more madly active than usual that summer. There
were thirty-odd ex-G.I.'s enrolled as students, and their presence
introduced a jocose sophistication into those hitherto quiet and
art-dedicated hills. When the last class of the day was over, my
car stood ready to take a group of these pleasure-hungry ex-
soldiers to the surrounding towns for movies, for drinks, for
dancing. My reference books remained unopened; my typewriter
stood closed. Always telling myself that any deadline that
couldn't be avoided could be met at the last minute with extra-
hard work, I managed to have a happy summer.

There were ten free days between the closing of the Pillow
and the opening of my own theater. In those ten days I sat at
my typewriter eight hours daily and completed my book on
Spanish dancing. After that I plunged back into the maelstrom
of lessons, rehearsals, and performances. I went on out-of-town
engagements alone or with an ensemble or company—to New
England, Florida, Wisconsin, and in between to the Brooklyn
Academy, the American Museum of Natural History, and back
again to my own demanding theater.

In the tumult of New York life I could not have relaxed if
I had tried. The classes, rehearsals, twice-a-week shows in my
own theater, and outside engagements averaging at least four a
month had become a regular schedule. Even so, I now found
myself seeking some new outlet.

I began to be more troubled than ever about the problem
of young dancers, especially those interested in ethnic dance, for
I felt their frame of performance was woefully limited and in-
adequate. There were companies that young dancers coming out
of ballet and modern-dance schools could join as fledglings. But
in the ethnic field there were few such companies and not many
New York stages where they could perform.

My best thinking has always been done while I am on tour.
Sitting in a car, I am free of the demands of a set schedule or of

the unexpected chores that somehow manage to drop into my
lap. So it was that while I was on a ten-day tour of the colleges
in Georgia in January 1947, I dreamed up my Young Artists
Series.

For this series I invited young artists of ethnic dance who
were working toward concert performances to appear in my
theater. I auditioned those whose work I had not yet seen so
that the standard of performance would be high in seriousness of
purpose and in talent. We offered these young people a good
stage, lit by Averardo; we offered them publicity, a Broadway
critic—when blessed Walter Terry could make it—and fifty percent of the gate. My resident group danced during the costume
changes in the Young Artists' performances, and the necessity of
producing group numbers to match those of the soloists kept us
jumping. For example, there was the time that Cebyn Dwaty
Mafaunwy, a Comanche Indian, danced with live snakes. What
had we to offer that would match that?

All told, in that first year I presented fourteen young un-
knowns, most of whom, given that springboard, went on to highly successful careers. Among them was Ira-Ari, a brilliant young
Brazilian and new arrival on our shores. A charming and beautiful girl, she was so enchanted with my resident group that she
decided to use it in a number of her own devising. Her English
being somewhat sketchy, she used to reduce the group to helpless
giggles when she cadenced her instruction with "one, two, three,
four, five, *sex*."

The year rushed by, crowded with activity—Morristown,
Atlantic City, Buffalo, Quincy, Worcester, Needham, Lowell,
Harrisburg, Detroit, Des Moines. There were times when we
presented a program at the museum in the afternoon and
another one at my theater in the evening. There were times
when we returned to New York at 6 P.M. and gave a performance
in the theater at 8. Sometimes our engagements were so far-
flung and dated so close together that I would fly ahead to give
a solo performance in one town and then fly off to another to
rejoin my troupe. Boston, Chicago, Springfield, Indianapolis,
Massilon—through floods, tornadoes, and blizzards we went. You

have to *like* to travel, you have to love the theater, and—somehow—you have to feel deeply that you are giving something of beauty and understanding to the people out front. It is that at least that keeps one at it. Believe me, for pure self-aggrandizement, it is not worth it. For that reason many give up after a very few years.

When summer came, I again offered an intensive course, managing to dash up to the Pillow for weekend performances. By September I was completely exhausted and determined to snatch a ten-day vacation in Bermuda.

I took Topsy with me, for Colonial Airlines said they would accept her if she were crated. Averardo knocked together a crate from an old orange box. Never have I seen a more unappreciative dog! Just before the plane took off, the handsome young pilot came back to my seat to tell me Topsy had broken out of her crate. But when he saw my distress at the thought of leaving her behind, he offered to take her up with him. So Topsy made her first flight riding up front with our pilot and, I imagine, peering down from time to time at the sunny sea beneath her.

We had an unforgettable holiday—Topsy and I. We swam together twice a day. I took endless bicycle trips with Topsy galloping beside me. And, gloriously tired, we sat in the garden, and I read poetry while my nerves unwound in the warm sunshine.

Our departure from Bermuda at the end of our stay was not without a small bit of drama. For some strange reason my entrance manifest read: Russell Carreras and daughter Topsy. Naturally the authorities insisted that when I left the island, I take my "daughter" with me! Fortunately, hastily phoned acquaintances assured the authorities that Topsy was a dog, *not* a daughter.

My little vacation in Bermuda rekindled my love for touring in foreign lands. Yet I was afraid to go it alone, nor was I in any financial position to hire a manager to act as buffer between me and the awesome paperwork involved in such jaunts. However, as the autumn, overfull with my usual tasks, unrolled, I became increasingly convinced that if I could once more regain that personal confidence I had always felt as an artist in a foreign land, I would know where I had erred in my "selling" relations with the dance world in New York.

During the next seven months I put by a small nest egg from the monies earned on tours and the Ethnic Dance Theater performances. I wrote my old friend Cabral in Lima. I made contact also with that dynamo of press relations, Fern Helscher. And in the spring of 1948, leaving a three-month plan of studio activity in the capable if overworked hands of Lilian, Averardo, and DiFalco (one of the G.I. bill students), I packed my costumes, took along my pupil Rebecca Harris, and enplaned for Mexico. Surely somewhere under the familiar Southern Cross I would find an answer to my tangled problems.

For this tour of Latin America I went back to my status as solo dancer. By now I had learned that the present movie-conditioned audience was not hospitable to waiting while the soloist changed costumes, so I carried with me three full programs of my "Onstage Dressing Room." This was a presentation I had already tried out on my own stage and on the proving ground of the Jacob's Pillow Dance Theatre. It consisted of a little dressing room with table and costume rack placed upstage center behind the cyclorama. At the end of each dance the cyclorama opened, and I went into this dressing room to change, chatting with the audience as I donned the next costume. Becky, dressed as a maid, helped me change, and with carefully routined movements she screened me with the larger portions of my costumes. In Latin America this posed an unexpected problem, for as I dressed, the backstage crew would stampede noisily upstage in the wings to peer behind our protective silks. The weeks I was there those stagehands got a lot of extra exercise!

Although I felt sure of an artistic welcome under the Southern Cross, I was uneasy as to the practical aspects, for I had never traveled internationally before without company management. In spite of my apprehensions, it was not managerial difficulties that roughened the way.

Though there was the usual tangle of red tape at the

Mexican border, we got through in good time for our performance in Monterrey. From there we took train for the capital. As we climbed into the rarified atmosphere of the high plateau, my teeth began to ache and I spent my first hours in Mexico City in a dentist's chair. I gave thirteen performances, sometimes two a day, met many charming people, saw many interesting things, but I could think of little else than my aching jaw. Three of the teeth became impacted. I could not eat anything and subsisted only on chocolate milks. I grew thin as a rail, yellow as a pumpkin. I had to take penicillin—I, who hate needles!—and in the end had to have all three teeth pulled out between performances. To say I was not dancing my best is a miracle of understatement. Happily for vanity and aesthetics, the teeth were all in the back. I left Mexico part-Mexican, thanks to my three new teeth.

My Mexican season over, I went to air-freight my costumes to Costa Rica. A bitter blow awaited me. The authorities would not let me send my costumes—*my* costumes—out of the country, claiming they belonged to Mexico—a sort of left-handed compliment to their authenticity. Then another difficulty arose. On her entrance questionnaire innocent Becky had stated that she entered the country by car. The authorities insisted we produce the car and take it with us when we left. For a few days it looked very much as if we'd have to apply for citizenship in the country before we could leave it.

Like the U.S. Marines, my ex-pupil Josefina came to the rescue. She introduced us to an American who had lived in Mexico for some years and knew all the ways. The car difficulty he solved by the simple expedient of erasing Becky's statement on the questionnaire. The costume difficulty he solved by hurrying me off in a plane for San Antonio with half my costumes "bootlegged" in a trunk under personal clothes. In Texas I transshipped those costumes to New York via the ubiquitous American Express and returned the same day to Mexico City. Then Becky and I booked passage on a plane going south, with the balance of my costumes hidden under a layer of dresses. For once in my life I felt relieved instead of afraid as the big airplane took to the skies. But all this shadowboxing had made it necessary to cancel our tour in Costa Rica. Now we were off to Panama.

The Panama season was wonderful. Every performance was a success, and the box office was a sellout. Backstage at the Municipal Theatre the stage crew remembered me and came to show me their collection of the programs for my 1928 season. Again I was in a land where the press linked my name favorably with the greats—Argentina, Argentinita, Pavlova, and the others.

In spite of a tense political situation everything went right. The governor general of the Canal Zone came to the opening with his entourage, and it was a signal for a round of festive entertainments. I drank deep of the exhilarating waters of professional glamour. And yet, whether I was dancing a rumba under the stars or swimming in my hostess's big outdoor pool, a sense of discord nagged at the back of my mind. Though I was too caught up in enjoying myself to stop to analyze it, something was wrong with my timing. An unexpected engagement in Ecuador momentarily drove away the shadowy cloud.

I had not been to Ecuador before. The stark contours of the country, the gentle, formal courtesy of its people enchanted me. Here life followed the more gracious patterns of an earlier era. Poets and their works were honored; the classics were read and studied at well-attended conferences. To my astonished delight I found my own limited efforts at verse known and respected. The local paper lacked bona fide dance critics, but several literary men were asked to review my concert. They requested permission to attend my rehearsal and asked me to explain the dances to them so that they might review them with knowledge. I felt myself once more in a world in which I was not a misfit in time, and it was very heartening.

Nevertheless, the defects of the mechanical age made themselves evident the night of my debut. As darkness fell and the lights in Guayaquil were turned on, our record player lost power and played my music at half time. The result was that the program ran far longer than was comfortable.

Before leaving Ecuador, I flew up to Quito in a tiny plane,

winging a bumpy way between towering and too-close Andean
peaks. But how beautiful the serene city with its sun-drenched
streets and quiet cathedrals where colorful Indians came and
went. One unforgettable day we arose at 3 A.M. to drive up to
the Otavalo fair. From far up in the mountains the Indians
came to exchange goods. They laid out their wares in a cold
outdoor market—hand-loomed wool in many colors, hard, chalked
felt hats, hammered silver jewelry, embroidered belts and blouses.
There was even an Andean version of a department for livestock,
vegetables, and fruits.

The Indians, a tall, handsome, laughing people, made us welcome and sold us their goods without venality, importunity, or
scorn. A small boy of about ten attached himself to us and
"protected" us from high prices and inferior goods. He showed
us where to go for lunch and even ordered for us. He begged us
to take him to the States; I so wished that I could.

Our flight along the Pacific coast gave me a new perspective on
the cliffs I had not seen from the air. Their towering grandeur is
awesome but from the air seems somehow gentler, and the sun
paints them in unbelievable colors. I felt relaxed by their
beauty, and by the time darkness blotted them out, I had begun
to enjoy the flight.

When we came over the bowl wherein lies the jewel of
Lima, we plunged into fog so thick that it was impossible to see
the leading edge of our wings; it was almost as if the fog were
some lost creature from another civilization, lonely and afraid,
pressing against our windows to find company.

I was not so sure that I liked flying after all. We circled
several times and went down for an instrument landing. An instant before the wheels touched ground, the diamond lights of
the city sprang out in the clear air. It had been, I was told, a
normal landing for Lima.

Señores Cabral and Gonzales met us at the airport. To our
surprise a courtly customs officer waved our luggage through unopened, and I was back, to my delight, in the lovely capital I
had visited for the first time in 1928. This was 1948, twenty
years later.

In our two weeks in Lima we gave seven concerts at the Municipal Theatre. I had hoped to fly up to Cuzco and Machu Picchu, but there was political unrest, and the airline would not sell us tickets.

There was no time to go on to Chile now. I was due back for a performance at the Pillow. So my tour was over by the end of July. I boarded a plane for home.

During the twenty-four-hour flight from Peru to New York I gingerly examined the unrest that had been nagging at me since I began the tour. In spite of the warm success my little tour had enjoyed, I felt sure that the era of the solo dancer was finished, abroad as well as in the States. With a changing world, the demands of the theater were changing. The booker, more interested in quantity than quality, was booking large companies carrying complete décor and using full orchestra. Wonder at the delicate shadings in the program of the creative soloist had worn thin. The new dance stage must be fully peopled. The single piano accompanist or the canned music of recordings was discarded in favor of a full orchestra in the pit. Perhaps this had been brought about by the influence of the "colossal" screen productions, or perhaps it was simply a natural evolution. The end result was frightening to contemplate. Where in future would the dancer find the financial means to meet these new demands? Government subsidy? Individual underwriters, a variation of the medieval patron system? Whatever, the creative soloist was facing a drastic revision of artistic conditions. And with young ones coming along, I knew I must change or perish.

Before I reached New York, I had faced up to this disturbing fact and had decided that in my ballet company lay our hope for the future. I must seek financial aid to broaden its scope, to buy décor, to pay musicians. Heretofore I had been unsuccessful in obtaining grants or any other form of subsidy. I would try again. Surely this time a way would open. I landed in New York inspired by a warm feeling of dedication.

My optimism was short-lived. I stepped into a studio where the very atmosphere was tense with countercurrents. The financial situation was a shambles.

In three short months the center had gone several thousand dollars into debt! Even the public utilities had not been paid. The need for bringing order out of this chaos appalled me. Mindful of the whole future as well as the clamorous present, I called on the scholarship students for help. They, at least, had been getting their salaries, small as they were, while Con Edison waited. The students had an even larger stake in the future than I. Surely they would see the point and rally round. I called a meeting of my company and put the cards on the table.

I met a blank wall. For some reason these inexperienced children were convinced that I was sitting on a pot of money and, for some reason of my own, was refusing to help extricate us from our plight. Youthfully confident of their individual talents, they believed that, in the circumstances, they would be better off each striking out on his own. They could not see, as I did, that now the only strength of the concert dancer lay in unity. They suspected that I was using them for my own self-interest. It was useless to try to show them the future as I saw it, a future in which only the big dance production would find acceptance. One by one they skittered away, until of my company of fifteen only three remained to "man the pumps."

In something of a panic I took any and all jobs I could get at any fee offered—television at $5 a day, lectures that netted $20—anything, including rummage sales of my costumes and records. In my innocent stupidity I was so embittered by this unexpected wrecking of my hopeful plans that I began to feel life not worth the living. As indeed she should have, my guardian angel fetched me the slap I needed to bring me out of incipient hysteria. Dr. Freed ordered me into the hospital!

I had been ill about half the time for nearly two years but never could seem to take the time to do anything about it. Finally, after an engagement upstate, my will to do was so nearly gone that even my work was a brutal drag; I went to see my doctor. He lectured me and took steps.

They give you some pills; they give you shots; and when they wheel you into the operating room, you are supposed, obligingly, to be out like a light. I fought it all the way.

Uncounted hours later a telephone rang at my bedside. "I just wanted to let you know, Dickie," said the doctor cheerily, "it isn't cancer." Too groggy still to be quite polite, I muttered, "I never even thought of that," and hung up.

My body having failed to make a simple, frank declaration, the next day we had it all over again. "Well," I remarked, bumping along on the car to the operating room, "after yesterday's rehearsal we ought to have a good show today." They overlooked me and my sorry quips and went to work again. I was scared to death. But my guardian angel—transformed now into Dr. Freed—knew what he was doing. The long slide down the anesthetic into nothingness was enough of a facsimile of dying to cure me forever of underselling the fact of being alive.

Contrary to medical instructions, I danced at a museum concert fifteen days after the operation and the following day took off on a southern tour. After all, why had I had the operation if not to make it possible for me to get back to my work?

With the dissolution of the Exotic Ballet Company, work in the center theater had slowed down appreciably. Lacking a company that was stabilized, the Young Artists Series had been abandoned, and our performances were cut down from four a week to about four a month. I had brought back fresh information from Latin America and two new dances, based on Otavalo and Peruvian works—*Yaravi,* a full ballet, and the duet suite, *Peruvian Dances.*

Occasionally we rented the theater to drama companies or dancers. But there was not enough theater work to keep my longtime friend, Averardo, busy. He finally capitulated to a decently paid job in keeping with his talents and left us.

The tours also suffered from our lack of a big company. But with an ensemble of three dancers plus my solo programs I averaged some thirty engagements during the winter months. All the hard-earned money from our road tours went into the upkeep of the center—rent, utilities, insurance, and so on. Since I understood only too well the financial problems of the dancer, my fees for lessons were kept absurdly low. Also many of my most talented pupils, lacking funds, were working on scholarships.

One hopeful sign, albeit a small one, was the rise of television. Gradually this was opening up a new field. We had worked in this medium since the days of its infancy, when pay was $5 a day and the lights were so hot that bare feet literally blistered from the floor. I had urged my youngsters to see to it that they were in on the ground floor, if only because changing choreographic techniques were obviously becoming necessary for the camera. Perhaps I should have taken my own advice, but I could not yet bring myself to jettison my center, the people who remained loyal to it, and the ideal upon which it was based. I still felt driven to give the sum of my knowledge in full measure to the oncoming generation of dancers. I wanted to pass on to them some means of survival in our machine age. They were even better equipped psychologically to fight the battle than I, with my outmoded mores of "dignity and honor and ethics," my years of "making love" to the warm, live audiences before me. How could I pour out my heart to the cold and fishy eye of the camera? How lose myself in my dance if I must watch for those limiting chalk marks on the floor? How shape into the V of the lens choreography designed for a full stage? For me, dance is an emotional duet between artist and audience; one cannot perform a duet alone. Yet here, I knew, was the financial solution for the contemporary dancer. There was no more vaudeville to replenish the empty coffers of the concert artist as there had been in the days of Denishawn. Even Broadway, which so often had saved dancers of my generation financially, had shrunk from some four hundred to some forty going theaters. The rest were empty or else their marquees announced live television shows.

Yet few of my young dancers deigned to turn to this medium, and I, the misfit, could not.

On the road even the ensemble was proving increasingly difficult to book at a profit. I decided to groom Di Falco as a partner so that we might travel in two and cut down on expenses. The last tour I made with the ensemble was a never-to-be-forgotten trip west during the record-breaking winter of 1949.

We were four in the car—two girls, one man, and myself. None

of us knew a gasket from a tire rim. I had been teaching Di Falco
to drive, but when the going got tough, I didn't dare trust him and
did the driving myself. We were in a new Ford station wagon, one
of those pregnant- type jobs that everyone was predicting would
fall to pieces on the first bad curve.

East of Denver the weather was fine, although storm warn-
ings were out all over the place and the AAA told us without
mincing words to stay where we were. But what does a Texan
know—or care—about snow and mountains? "Is anybody going
through?" we demanded. If so, why couldn't we? So we
climbed up into the Rockies, pausing a moment to watch skiers
in Berthoud Pass. On the other side of the pass the sun went
away, a wind blew up, and snow came down in the order named.
Where could one go but on?

Nature worked herself into a grand tantrum that had its
climax at Rabbit Ears Pass. The landscape was littered with
stuck cars, buses, trucks, and snowplows. It was snowing and
blowing so hard I could hardly see the radiator cap, let alone
the road. So Di Falco, in low-cut shoes, light topcoat, and no
hat, got out and walked backward ahead of the car, waving his
arms to show me where the road was. The windshield wiper
froze. Every three minutes Di Falco, the color of purple cab-
bage, would get into the car for a minute to thaw out. In the
snowy whiteness all other wheeled traffic was blanked out. We
seemed the last living inhabitants of an utterly unknown
civilization.

Again I asked myself, where could we go but on? Again
Di Falco did battle with the elements, though if he got more
than two feet ahead of the car, I could not see him at all.

Almost imperceptibly the snow began to let up. When we
finally cleared the pass, I could see the road once more. We
eased down the icy curves. Stopped by a couple of stranded
cars, we promised to send a wrecker from Steamboat Springs.
We tried to stop at a farmhouse to call a wrecker for them by
phone, but we fell into a snowbank, and when we had clawed
our chainless way out, I was too frightened to stop again. At
Steamboat Springs we were the only vehicle rolling. Not until

two hours after we got there did other cars begin limping down from the pass; some just sat it out in the pass all night.

From Steamboat Springs to Craig was rough driving, but the air was clear and sunny without much wind. We pushed on to Maybell, but the pass over the mountains was blocked, so we turned back to spend the night in Craig, Maybell being little more than a wide place in the road. It was some thirty miles from Maybell to Craig. Trucks had gouged out tracks, but on the way a new storm struck. For two hours we sat in one place in snow so thick we couldn't see anything but each other. Finally the wind slackened a little. Behind and ahead of us, companions in misery sat in cars, snow drifted over their wheels. For three more hours we slogged forward in low, backed up, pushed other cars, and were pushed by them. Hungry, frightened, sore from fighting a bucking steering wheel, we finally got back to Craig at six. Too nervous to go to bed early, we dropped into a movie. And what did we see? Palm trees, beaches of white sand, girls in sarongs with big red flowers behind their ears! I nearly wept!

The next morning I awoke at 4:30 and began to worry. All morning we drifted from the bus terminal to the highway patrol post, trying to learn of an open highway to Salt Lake City. We hit the road again at 1 P.M. It was clear in most places, and we made it back to Maybell in an hour. But there even the rotary plow was stuck, so we drove back to Craig. I began to feel like the shuttle train between Grand Central Station and Times Square!

The day was long and wearisome. Some of our party suggested that we stop fooling around and take the only road open—the one to Denver—and go home. But, remembering the code of mailmen, doctors, and show people, I wouldn't hear of it!

At six in the morning of the next day we set out for Maybell again. It was clear and still—and thirty below zero! In Maybell a huge truck driver flagged us down. "You can't get through," he told us matter-of-factly. "They're *all* stuck up on the mountain, even the snowplow. In this weather the gas lines are freezing up."

"But if I start," I said, "is there room to turn around and come back if I have to?"

He eyed me with disgust. "Lady, there's nothing up there but room—room and snow and dead automobiles." He added thoughtfully, "The patrol isn't going up there anymore today. So—you go up there, and you'll sure be on your own."

I was sick of commuting between Craig and Maybell so I pointed the Ford westward.

I drove and I drove. All along the road were the abandoned "bones" of cars and trucks and even animals. The road was fairly clear, but all around us there was a weird absence of any signs of life. No house, no moving thing, no living man. Just us and the snow and God. We all were mighty quiet. I began to realize how much depended on any one of the hundreds of wires inside that engine hood. My stomach tied up in knots, my chin trembled uncontrollably.

And all of a sudden there was a house!

Di Falco slogged off to it to beg a glass of water so I could take an Empirin to steady me. He brought back the welcome news that we were over the worst of the way. I must say the road didn't look any different to me, just a winding ribbon of phantomlike, blinding whiteness. However, hope renewed, we all began to speak to each other again.

The car began to cough a little, but we sighted a town a-head, the first since leaving Maybell. In Vernal, Utah—Vernal, yet!—we left the car in a garage for repair while we went for lunch. We stopped at the bus terminal for the latest information. "How are the roads out?"

"West, it's clear to Heber. East, the road is closed."

"Closed? We just came through from the east."

They closed in around us and gaped. You could see they didn't believe us.

"We just got a phone call that the road is completely im-passible," they said, somewhat reprovingly. "Fifty cars are stuck, mostly with froze-up gas lines, and there's been no patrol on that road for twenty-four hours." A slight snicker ran around the knot of bystanders. *That'd* nail our lie!

Back at the garage they were still skeptical but not quite so blunt about it. They said they didn't see how we'd made it. Peering into the car's innards, they muttered too about wiring points and condenser—whatever those were.

To us Utah looked cold and empty, yet awfully good. We still had Strawberry Pass to make, and they'd been telling us since Kansas that *that* road had been closed all winter.

Well, the road was winding and windy, all right, ledge-steep and covered with ice. But after our morning's experience, it seemed quite cheery, since every half-hour or so we'd see signs of life—a car, a snowplow, a man, a house.

At 4:30 we sighted beautiful Salt Lake City. A half-hour later we were safely within its limits. Ten hours of driving—and I do mean *driving*! We were the only transportation to arrive in that city in twenty-four hours. No trains, no cars, no buses, no planes. We felt as intrepid as Byrd at Little America!

Our sponsor greeted us with pleased surprise, certainly not expecting us to put in an appearance. Yet the sequel to our stupidly courageous effort was bitterly amusing. We gave two performances in one day. After the evening show the sponsor came backstage, and, first praising our performance, he informed us that he was not paying us inasmuch as our advance publicity had stated "five peoples" and we were only four! In vain did I explain that five *peoples* meant that the dances on our program pertained to five peoples, or races, or nations. The upshot was that we had to go to law. We waited six months to get paid for that little flight of determination! As I always say, there's no business like show business.

In May of the following summer Di Falco and I crossed Rabbit Ears Pass again en route to California. The world was green and sunny. No snowstorm hid the view. The road wound precariously in and out among the mountains, which leaped precipitously upward on one side of us and fell into breathtaking gorges on the other. We shuddered to think we had driven this ridiculously narrow life line in the blizzard, and we offered up our grateful tribute to the destiny that had nodded to us, letting us pass.

Di Falco and I had been working for some time as a team and now were on our way to some west-coast engagements, one of which was to teach master classes in Miss Ruth's studio. I was so looking forward to seeing her again, to sitting at her feet, to drawing on her wisdom for help in solving my own problems.

We found her unchanged, beautiful as always, dynamic, filled with her plans for the future. In a long hour of confiding talk I poured out my woes: "My company is gone. Soon I shall have to close my theater, for the fire department has demanded more alterations than I can afford. My school as such does not cover the expenses of its upkeep. Touring is becoming all but impossible and a good deal less than well paid. But I cannot bear to give it all up. Where am I to turn?"

"Of course you cannot give it up, my dear," said Miss Ruth serenely. "Don't be silly. You were born to work, just as I was. And work we will—to the death and beyond. But you must be practical too. There are so many ways of managing. Have you thought of them all? There are so many ways of taking a fortress . . . the siege, the attack, the sapping under. Now you want to go on giving of your knowledge. Indeed I have watched you—you *must* go on giving it. But it need not be from *behind* the footlights."

"I see," I said doubtfully, not at all sure that I saw. "But you know—well, there is always the thing of making a sort of living. There's money . . ."

"Oh, that!" Miss Ruth waved a delicate hand. "You cannot be thinking about that or you will get nowhere. Besides, that would be *selling*, and *you* have to *give*. Think about ways in which you will *give*. You will see. It will be all right."

So I thought about it. *To give.* To give *knowledge and inspiration.* But the key word was *knowledge.* All else would take off from there. The theater in my country might be floundering, but everyone was interested in knowledge, in learning. A college diploma was almost as common as a high school certificate had once been.

Very well, then. I would storm the fortress of the future with what I had to offer those who would learn from me. Suddenly I was happy again. I had a new dream, a new hope, new plans to make.

An End and a Beginning

On my return trip eastward that summer of 1949 I stopped off at Iowa State University to teach for a month. At this juncture in my affairs the offer from the university was so fortuitous that it seemed like a nod of approval from a benign destiny.

It was my first experience in the field of higher education, for I held no degree and my two somewhat slapdash years of college study were in the far-distant past. I plunged in, haunted the library between my classes and quizzed fellow teachers on a range of pedagogical approaches in this field that was so new to me.

In my dance center background lectures had already become regular fare for my students, but on my return to New York I added to the already overloaded schedule, making such study compulsory for those dancers who elected to go for a three- or four-year course. In forty-five hours of classes a week they took not only dance techniques but the study of ethnic dance— history and culture as well as choreography, music fundamentals, pedagogy, and costume design.

They were required to keep notebooks, to do outside research. They were given a short course in public speaking and twice a year took stiff oral and written examinations. Upon the satisfactory completion of their elected three- or four-year course, they were given a certificate and also gave a public solo appearance on a selected stage. In spite of the fact that I could never manage to get my school approved for inclusion in the credit system, our standard was so high that several of my graduates found the little piece of paper that was their certificate a means of opening doors in accredited schools.

When the full curriculum was first introduced in the fall of 1949, many students, appalled, elected to study only dance techniques. But there were hardier, hungrier souls who plunged in and fought through to the end.

In spite of the heavy study schedule, I did not give up touring or the engagements in and around New York. Indeed, financially I dared not. True to my karma, all my idealistic plans were going forward beautifully, though my financial problems were as grave as ever.

Then began the years that, in slow diminuendo, saw the shrinking frame of presentation for the ethnic dancer. Suddenly, almost without warning, the American Museum of Natural History's ethnic-dance series closed. Hazel Miller had started the series in the early forties. The first performance, which presented me in a group of Latin American dances, was given in the Hall of Birds, the audience such people as chanced to be visiting the museum that afternoon. Over the years the series had grown and been shifted to the main auditorium. In little more than a decade the prestige value of the series had grown to the point where the finest ethnic dancers were appearing: Shankar, Antonio, Rey, Tei Ko, and many others, not forgetting Ted Shawn and Ruth St. Denis.

Yet with all this fine and still growing success, with full houses out front and great artists on the stage, the powers that be decided the series was not making enough money and with a stroke of the pen signed its death warrant. Since it was wholly an ethnic series and I and my dancers had always appeared several times each season, we were hard hit by the closure.

Next, inexplicably, the Joseph Mann series petered out. This series, which had fought a magnificent battle for modern dance in its formative years, had presented all the finest artists and for many years had a huge subscription following. In spite of its preference for the modern dance, I had often appeared on the Mann series in works of a purely creative nature as against the traditional dances preferred by the museum series. Mr. Mann stood staunchly for the avant-garde in dance, and it was on his stage that I presented my abstract creative works based on ethnic techniques.

What was happening to the dance world? These two long-established and highly respected dance series had died within a year of each other. Was television luring away the audience? Were the increasingly hard-to-please critics discouraging the young dancers? Or was a postwar America finding money too tight to spend on culture?

Lacking my own theater to house my creative work, I turned my interest to creating for Theatre Dance, Inc., and the Choreographers' Workshop. I did not appear in these works myself, for I was aware of the swiftly narrowing field open to young dancers.

Under the frighteningly expert eye of Louis Horst we auditioned to acceptance my *Sinfonia Menuda,* a group work accompanied only by the performers' castanets and heel beats. I also re-created the *Yaravi* and the *Bach-Bharata,* the latter with Di Falco in the solo role instead of myself. But some strange malign force was still at work, and presently these two choreographic-presentation societies ceased to exist.

In spite of these deaths from malnutrition, Jacob's Pillow still functioned in the Berkshires, proud, strong, and growing. Summer after summer I went up there to teach and to appease my creative hunger with works on its marvelous stage. In 1950 I did Turina's *Danzas Fantasticas*; in 1951, when I created *Debussy Suite,* I also appeared in Ted Shawn's new ballet, *Song of Songs.* It was a fearsome week for me, as it happened, for in an unguarded moment Shawn told me he had first conceived the role for Miss Ruth, news which was no help to me at all, for *who* can be Miss Ruth but Miss Ruth?

In the fall Shawn booked a tour for the Jacob's Pillow Dance Festival Company, a distinguished group. I was included. It was a long tour and not an easy one—fifty cities in two months. I did not mind the work and the traveling. I never have. But two months was too long to be away from my new academy, and I was brought up again against the fact that I just could not be in two places at once—on the road making money to support the center and in the center, teaching and directing.

Again I did some hard soul-searching. I believed in my

center and in its artistic and educational value. Yet it was haunted by debt, and it seemed that only my outside work could keep it afloat. I had to choose which road to take, and, against Miss Ruth's injunctions, I *had* to think of money! All my years of experience had not expunged my faith that the world would beat a path—bringing its pocket money!—to the door of the maker of the better mouse trap.

In the summer of 1953 I let my academic students go on holiday and went for a ten-week stay at Jacob's Pillow. It was a brilliant season. Besides a couple of weeks when I danced solos and duets with Di Falco, there was, for the first time in the history of the Pillow, a week of an all-ethnic program. Bill topper was the de Falla *Amor Brujo,* which I choreographed and which was danced by Shawn, Goya, Di Falco, Lilian, and myself with a group. I also choreographed a tone poem for myself and four dancers to Vivaldi's *The Seasons.* That week was terribly hard work but eminently satisfying. I was particularly happy about the Vivaldi work, for it was a long step forward in conception, going even further away from the traditional than my *Bach-Bharata.*

I was elated with audience and critical reaction. But the cherry on the cake came when Antony Tudor, greatest of ballet choreographers and never one to give compliments lightly, gave it his unqualified approval. Whatever else I have or have not gained in my life, these are my riches—the approval of such towering figures as Tudor, Coomaraswamy, Argentinita, Pearl Buck, Kreisler, Respighi, and others like them.

Lest you who read this think that the life of an artist is all exotic happenings, I must at this point disillusion you. We have all the ordinary troubles plus a heavy portion of those that are intramural. Now, as a balance for my "exotic and glamorous" life, I was stricken—inexplicably—with a case of the itch! Doctors cried "allergy!" but it eluded all manner of pills and shots. My poor body, overworked for twenty-five years, broke out all over. I could not sleep at night and would burst into tears at the slightest provocation—or no provocation at all. For nearly two years I fought this undignified and hysterical disease before, most grudgingly, I gave up and admitted that, in all probability, it was hair dye that was the villain of the piece and I would have to let my hair do what it wanted to—grow out white.

For a woman leading an ordinary life this would have posed no problem. For a theater woman it meant an entirely new problem in the handling of my stage appearances—indeed, a new approach to living. A wig? Not with the *intime* and "for real" type of performances I presented! Gray hair? Not unless I changed my repertoire drastically. Who would believe in a steaming gitana or a gay olapa with gray locks?

In February of 1954 Di Falco and I started on the last tour of our well-booked ethnic-dance program. When I returned to New York, I planned to forswear my little bottle of hair dye. Then we should be able to tour no more as a team, for Di Falco was on the sunny side of thirty, and with gray hair I would look like his grandmother! I told him about it on our last long tour. We had arrived in Albuquerque, ignominiously towed by a wrecker after five searing hours in a black dust storm.

"Peter, I've had it!" I said bluntly. "I am tired of driving through floods and snowstorms and hurricanes—this dust storm is the last straw! From here on in, it's all yours. You're young; you can take it. Get yourself another partner or a little company. I hand you the torch. *You* carry it!"

So when we returned to New York late in March, we sold our station wagon; I packed away my ethnic costumes and set myself to solve the practical problems. For me, everything—but everything—had to be divided by the common denominator of money. With my little income I could live on an exceedingly modest basis, but I certainly could not support the center. To keep the school going I would have to have outside work. But as diligently as I explored the possibility of subventions, as obviously was I signally lacking in the skill to find that kind of capital. Well, what kind of outside work could I do that would admit of my gray hair? Lecture tours? I had done them; they pay so little that one must keep going incessantly in order to make any money. It is a strange thing, but nothing seems to frighten off the general public like the sound of the word

lecture. No, I couldn't count on lecture tours to save the
school. Besides, it would be the old story of having to be out
of town so much of the time that I couldn't spend enough time
in the school to keep *it* going.

Choreography? Few indeed were the companies that recognized the universality of appeal inherent in the ethnic techniques.
True, I had done choreography for Slavenska, Federico Rey,
Carola Goya, but this was "sometime" work, wonderful to do
but not continual enough to count on for support. There were
royalties from records and my dance books, but these would be
mere drops of water poured into an ocean. Serious art seldom
has been a good financial investment, and it would seem now
that its stock was plummeting daily.

With so many avenues closed, I contemplated the rocky
road of commercial "show biz." At this desperate moment it
was surely worth a try. So I spent several months working out
an evening's entertainment with a fine concert pianist. As a
theme I took the story of my career. For laughs—that commodity
so prized by American audiences—I would relate my experiences
during my studies in foreign lands, dramatizing myself as a stupid
one who could not comprehend anything. I would wear glamorous evening dresses, using only castanets for props and scarves
for the dances themselves. It seemed as if it could not miss, and
with unflagging optimism I pictured myself as the Victor Borge
of the dance.

Studio previews and New England break-ins strengthened
my belief that I had got hold of something. But I reckoned
without the "moving finger" that had written me large on the
minds of the New York dance field as an erudite and serious
artist. Too many influential persons were disturbed by my
laughing at myself. Theater business liked the idea and wanted
to book me into supper clubs. But I doubted my ability to hold
an audience without floodlights between us; supper-club work
needs a very special approach and takes years of experience, just
as does stage experience.

My "Little Show," therefore, failed to save the center
financially.

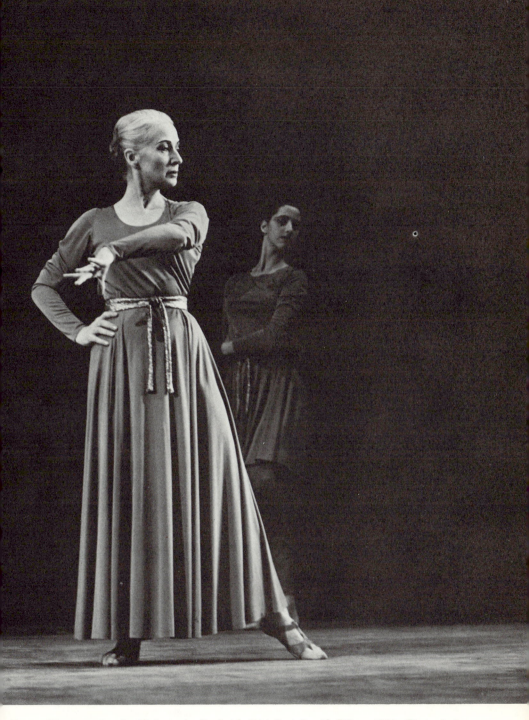

Escape (Choreography, La Meri; music, Frederick Bristol) at Jacob's Pillow, 1960. (Photo during performance: Jack Mitchell)

Parvati in *Pradakchina of Ganash* (Choreography, La Meri), 1969. This was the last time I danced. (Photo: Craig, Cape Cod, 1969)

Very depressed, I just hung in there for two years doing whatever presented itself—extension-course classes at Teachers College;
workshops at the University of Texas, Oklahoma College for Wom-
en, Texas Womens College, New York University, and Boston
Dance Circle; writing for three encyclopedias; choreography for
Julliard and some dance companies; lectures here and there; and
the first run-through of this book. But all that was not enough. I
have never been a party person, my only interests being the theater
and nature. Hard put to it to pay my rent, I could not afford
theater tickets, and, I must say, my visits to feed the squirrels in
Central Park were a pale fillip of nature, more frustrating than
satisfying. Obviously I had a bad case of the bends, which was
bringing bitterness in its wake. And bitterness I can do without.

So in the late winter of 1959 I sold twenty years of accumulated company costumes and paraphernalia, and my sister
and I moved to Cape Cod.

For five years I kept myself relatively busy with master
classes (as far west as Missouri and Iowa), writing a couple of
books and commuting to summer classes at the Pillow. Best of
all, I had treated myself to a fine Belgian Sheepdog puppy and
began making the east-coast dog shows. It was a kind of choreography for me, and my instructor, Mary Dillaway, nearly went
out of her mind trying to change my series of *jetés* into the long
lope necessary for showing a large dog. I am very happy to
state that Micki Mi Bingen went through to her championship in
the summer of 1964.

My sister Lilian was taken ill in the fall of 1964 and died in
January 1965. In spite of Micki Mi and her puppies, the house
became very big and silent.

Since our arrival on the Cape Lilian and I had been very in-
active members of the Barnstable Comedy Club, a semiprofes-
sional group of actors of fifty years' standing and with their own
small theater. I began giving exercise classes, gratis, for this or-
ganization. Of course I could not leave it at that. I had five
talented young dancers studying with me in the daytime, so,
theater-minded me, I had to put on a full-length production with
five good amateurs and a dozen ladies who had never danced

before in their lives. It took all winter, for I made all the costumes myself.

I produced, choreographed, and costumed three of these
ethnic-dance evenings, and we built an audience for ethnic dance.
The bell had rung and the old fire horse was off again at full
gallop. With some sympathetic friends I incorporated the
Ethnic Dance Arts in January of 1970.   .

All winter I teach classes, grooming a small group of young
dancers into a repertory company that tours New England. In
the summer we give an ethnic-dance festival that presents concerts by the foremost ethnic-dance companies available, plus a
three-week workshop from which several students have stepped
into professional companies.

Given a little luck, health-wise, I will be doing this until my
final curtain falls.

E.D.A. is beset with pretty much the same problems that
dogged E.D.C.—pinching economy; the giving of full scholarships;
the training of a good dancer for three or four years, only to
lose her (him) to matrimony or another company; and always,
me doing most of the work. But this is my third start-at-the-
beginning, and I have become accustomed.

Besides, I chose this road myself and chose the horse to
ride it. No wooden carousel steed, he! The unpredictable, pied
mustang branded "ethnic dance" has given me a wild-running,
hard-bucking ride—but I did catch a few brass rings.

THE STAR ROPER

I'll throw my rope on a mustang star
    And if my loop falls true
I'll strap a surcingle over his back
    And we'll buck down the moonlit blue.

And if I can break him to ride him right
    So he'll know my hand on the rein
And will answer my whistle and heed my voice
    With a toss of his star-dust mane,

Then the Pegasus horse with his silver wings
  Can travel, for all I care,
On the white north wind to Parnassus top
  And trumpet the high, thin air.

For I'll ride my star to eternity's end
  And the music of the spheres
Shall echo the tune of his silver hoofs
  For the staves of a thousand years.

(San Antonio, 1920)

Index